1977

Five Plays from the Children's Theatre
Company of Minneapolis

Five Plays from the Children's Theatre Company of Minneapolis

edited by

John Clark Donahue

and

Linda Walsh Jenkins

UNIVERSITY OF MINNESOTA PRESS, MINNEAPOLIS

Printed in the United States of America
at the North Central Publishing Company, St. Paul

Published in Canada by Burns & MacEachern Limited, Don Mills, Ontario

Library of Congress Catalog Card Number 73-91051
ISBN 0-8166-0711-7

Acknowledgments

The Rockefeller Foundation's support and encouragement of the Children's Theatre Company in the compiling and preparation of these scripts are most gratefully acknowledged. Among the individuals whose assistance and collaboration have been important in making this volume possible are Gerald Drake, Timothy Mason, and Jan Archerd of the Children's Theatre Company; Arlen Snesrud, music copyist; and John and Robert Jenkins.

J. C. D.
L. W. J.

Contents

Halftones follow each play. Color photographs follow page 142.

The Children's Theatre Company: Then and Now

The Children's Theatre Company of the Minneapolis Society of Fine Arts began in 1965 as a handful of professional artists and performers who wished to create works of theater for young people. Since that time, guided by artistic director John Clark Donahue, the theater has grown into an organization which employs a full-time staff of nearly fifty, involves over a hundred young people in its educational programs and productions, and reaches an audience of over 100,000 annually. Throughout its development the company's goal has been the creation of theater of the finest quality for young people and their families — theater that implements the same standards in writing, acting, music, design, and direction as audiences expect to find in outstanding theater for adults.

This philosophy, and the rapid expansion and diversification of the programs that have resulted from it, have drawn considerable attention to the Children's Theatre Company. For instance, in 1972 the company presented an experimental children's production by Donahue at the Association Internationale de Théâtre pour l'Enfance et la Jeunesse (ASSITEJ), the international congress of theater for children and youth, in Montreal and Albany. The production, which provoked a certain amount of controversy, served to introduce the Minneapolis company to an international audience. In 1973 Donahue and his company received the American Theatre Association's Jennie Heiden Award for "excellence in professional children's theater." In 1974 the Children's

Theatre Company moved into its new multi-million-dollar theater complex — one of the most extensive facilities of its kind dedicated to theater and theater education for young people — where for the first time the company's classrooms, offices, technical shops, auditorium, and auxiliary stage facilities could be housed under one roof.

The five plays in this volume were created by the company and its playwrights during these years of growth, and consequently the scripts have a history that is closely bound up in the history of the Children's Theatre Company itself.

The concept that ultimately became the Children's Theatre Company began to evolve in 1962, when John Clark Donahue, a young painter, actor, and art teacher, started to work with the Moppet Players of Minneapolis, a children's theater group led by Beth Linnerson. When Donahue joined the small company, it was only a year old. The Moppet Players were adult and child volunteers who combined their skills in creative dramatics and improvisation to develop children's plays in which both adults and children participated as actors. At first they performed in a back room donated by Mama Rosa's, a restaurant in the West Bank community near the University of Minnesota. Then they moved into a building that had once housed a police station, and they obtained shop facilities in the neighborhood. Donahue was soon writing and directing for the Moppet Players as well as serving as their technical director and designer; he became artistic director of the company in 1964.

During these years Donahue's dual orientation toward painting and the theater found a challenging outlet in the possibilities of theater for children, and he began to formulate his dream of a new theater company that could create works on a much larger scale than that available to the Moppets. Ideological conflicts led to a split in the company, and Donahue and John Davidson, the managing director of the Moppets, went in search of a new artistic home. They found one at the Minneapolis Institute of Arts, and in 1965 the Children's Theatre Company opened its first season of plays there.

The Institute agreed to allow the company to use its 646-seat auditorium and a cubicle of office space for a year; if the theater drew as large an audience there as the Moppets had drawn at Mama Rosa's, the group could stay longer. With five productions that year (forty performances in all), the company drew an audience of 28,548, significantly beyond the 10,000 who had managed to squeeze into the back room at Mama Rosa's.

At this point only a few adults on the theater's staff received any salary, the shop facilities were still in their original location several miles away, and the plays were presented in an auditorium that was built for lectures, not for theater. A tiny projection room at the back of a small balcony in the auditorium had to do for the light and sound booth. The stage had a proscenium width of slightly more than twenty-six feet, a shallow forestage, a depth of only twelve feet behind the proscenium, and no fly space. Like the stage itself, the wing spaces were far from ideal, and the only backstage area was a narrow corridor which served as dressing room, makeup area, costume and prop storage, stage manager's office, and greenroom. It was here that the dozens of adults, teenagers, and children who performed the plays spent the frenetic hours offstage. (Donahue frequently used relatively large casts — for instance, some of the plays in this volume involve as many as sixty actors — and the dramatic effect of a large cast performing on a very small stage eventually became a trademark of the company's work.)

Despite the cramped conditions, the Children's Theatre Company flourished. A gallery that connected with the backstage hallway was converted for the company's use, new shop facilities were found nearby, classrooms were rented from a parochial school, and additional office and school space was secured in old houses in the neighborhood. Except for the addition of a small orchestra pit, a new sound and light booth, and an extension to the forestage, however, the physical facilities remained virtually unchanged through the 1972–73 season, which was the last full season in the auditorium.

When the Children's Theatre Company was first formed in 1965, the entire staff could sit at a very small table for a quiet discussion. In 1969 the staff members still met weekly in a small office, but the space was becoming more and more crowded as new members were added; eventually they were forced to move across the hall to a larger room. That move represented the beginning of a new phase of growth — the good old days were gone forever. The period from 1965 to "the move across the hall" was a time of growth by accretion with few real obstacles to hinder it. Donahue gradually added new members to his company — a technical director, costumers, a box-office manager, stage managers, and acting personnel, who would at times double as technicians, secretaries, or bookkeepers. Numerous staff members acted in the shows, taught classes to students, and served in administrative capacities. A typical work week was seventy hours long, and the salary range for nine months was between $3,000 and $5,000. (By 1974 the salary figures had nearly doubled, and the work year was nearly twelve months long.) Most of those on salary were company members who had already worked with the group for years as volunteers, and some were young adults who had begun with the company as children in Moppet days. Then, as now, volunteers of all ages auditioned for parts in the shows or worked on the stage crews. It was Donahue's aim to gather into the company people who were firmly committed to theater for children and who would become part of a permanent ensemble.

In 1968 the company's budget for the season was still only $77,350, but out of this budget the group was staging over one hundred performances (including weekday shows for school groups) for an audience that had grown to more than 50,000. At the same time the company was expanding and involving guest artists from the Twin Cities area in the plays. By 1973 the company had become a third partner (with the Institute of Arts and the College of Art and Design) in the Minneapolis Society of Fine Arts, and John Donahue was named an associate director of the organization. In recognition of the company's new autonomy its name was changed to the Children's Theatre Company of the Minneapolis Society of Fine Arts. The company's budgets became multiples of the earlier ones, and the Society of Fine Arts assumed a greater portion of the company's deficits. An important catalyst in the company's growth was the availability of outside funding, which by the 1970s had become a critical component in the increased scope of the company's activities.

One of the first organizations to provide substantial grant aid was the Minnesota state arts council. Although the arts council was still a fledgling in 1968, it made possible the company's summer classes for teenagers that year and the expansion of the summer school program the following year. It was in this way that the Children's Theatre School was established. Determined not to lose the impetus of the highly successful summer classes in 1969, Donahue asked staff members to teach classes on weekday afternoons during the normal school year on a volunteer basis. In cooperation with the Minneapolis public schools the staff developed a pilot project in which teenagers at selected inner-city schools were chosen by audition to take classes in the performing arts for academic credit on time released from their home schools. That first fall the staff members received no pay for teaching or administrating ten class-hours a week for thirty students, but the program's success was recognized by a $25,000 support grant from the National Endowment for the Arts and by the continued cooperation and assistance of the Minneapolis public schools, which provided bus service and partial funding. The NEA funding of the theater school was renewed for four consecutive years thereafter.

The Children's Theatre School also contributed to the establishment of the Minneapolis urban arts program, which was funded by a federal grant for innovation in arts education. As a part of the urban arts program, the theater school eventually attracted nearly one hundred students from area schools with courses in subjects as diverse as modern dance, ballet, African dance, pantomime, karate, fencing, yoga, voice and singing, music theory, acting, improvisation, technical theater, Japanese gardening, and concert band. In addition to attending classes in theater skills, the students took part in company productions and created small shows of their own.

Despite its experimental beginnings, the Children's Theatre School soon came to be recognized as an accredited performing arts teaching center for metropolitan teenagers. Artists and teachers from the theater company continued to be active in developing workshops and related programs throughout the Twin Cities area. In 1973 the company began to combine its two main functions of education and performance in a new program of residencies throughout Minnesota and the region. The theater had initiated a series of annual state tours in 1970 and had conducted a national tour in 1972; since the company had already successfully developed its touring capabilities, the first residencies were demonstrations and workshops offered in conjunction with two touring productions. The week-long residencies were conducted at schools in Minnesota, Iowa, and South Dakota. The program also extended the educational activities of the company to the college level; in a residency at St. Olaf College in Northfield, Minnesota, the touring group helped to shape a one-semester course around a ten-day period of workshops, seminars, and performances.

Grants from national and local sources also helped to develop another aspect of the company's work: the production of plays for adults and teenagers. These plays — classics, original productions, and experimental works — gave the performing ensemble the opportunity to work with new artistic challenges, thus opening additional possibilities for personal artistic growth among the company members. The adult plays also increased the visibility of the company in the community, which in turn brought prestige to the organization and attracted new audiences to the children's plays.

In 1971 the National Endowment for the Arts provided $25,000 in support of two such productions — Molière's *Le Bourgeois Gentilhomme*, in a new translation by John Lewin, and *Jerusalem*, an original work by Frederick Gaines. The grant was used to commission the translation, to hire additional actors, dancers, singers, and musicians from the community to perform in the productions along with the company staff, and to absorb some of the costs of materials and equipment for staging the plays. The grant also enabled the company to keep the ticket prices for the productions within reach of teenagers' budgets.

The largest boost from an outside source to the long-term development of the Children's Theatre Company came in 1970 with the Rockefeller Foundation's generous contribution of $250,000 in the form of a three-year grant. This was the first substantive support the foundation had ever given to a theater for children. As part of its program of arts funding, the foundation had investigated the possibility of giving "seed money'' to the Children's Theatre Company because the group appeared to have the ability to produce artistically excellent theater for children, teenagers, and their families and to create new plays for all age groups. The breadth of the audience served by the company was one factor that set it apart from the many theater groups which produce plays almost exclusively for adults or for children. (At performances of the Children's Theatre Company it is not unusual to see, for instance, two grandmothers — often without any accompanying children — enter the auditorium, followed in turn by teenagers or college students on a date, families, and a Scout troop.)

The Rockefeller Foundation stipulated that the seed money be used to promote overall growth, not to pay operating costs or regular staff salaries. In other words, the company had to use the funds to diversify its programs and to explore artistic and educational opportunities in ways that otherwise would have been beyond the range of its budget. With the aid of the grant the company began to expand its existing programs and to organize new ones. Another large portion of the subsidy was used to finance the participation of guest artists and the writing of new plays for both young people and adults. The Rockefeller Foundation, acknowledging the fact that the production of original plays is a financially risky undertaking, had earmarked some of the grant specifically for this purpose. The backing allowed the company to produce Donahue's *A Wall* (an adult play based on a scenario by Alvin Greenberg) and *The Cookie Jar*, among other new plays, without being totally dependent on box-office receipts to meet costs. The funding also enabled the company to assemble scripts and to document their creation as well as to explore the possibilities of embarking on creative work in various media.

The effectiveness of the new programs and other activities made possible by the Rockefeller funding became evident in the years that followed, and in the summer of 1972 the foundation lent additional support of a different nature. In a departure from its usual policy of not financing ''bricks and mortar'' projects the foundation contributed $500,000 toward the construction of the company's new theater and classroom complex. The foundation also provided a grant of $100,000 in 1974 to help the company absorb the interim expenses it incurred during the transition to the new facilities.

Despite the proliferation of the company's programs, the central focus of its activities continues to be its productions for children. In the 1969–70 season the company began to develop plays for very young children (eight years and under) to complement its productions for older children. These productions, which are taken on tour in the state annually, represent another aspect of the company's diversification. While all of the children's plays produced within a given season differ from one another in period, design, style, and content, most of them share a number of characteristics. Donahue's dynamic use of large casts has already been mentioned; the sets teem with action and color, creating a genuine sense of spectacle. The sets are often multilevel with two or three entrances on each side which make possible strong diagonal movement and surprising appearances and disappearances. Music, usually performed live by a small orchestra, is an integral part of all the plays. The scenes are carefully and precisely choreographed, and the action flows cinematically from one scene to the next. Lighting, a crucial element in the productions, is used extensively to evoke images as well as to illuminate the stage. (Donahue's directing techniques are discussed in greater detail in a collection of his plays entitled *The Cookie Jar and Other Plays*, edited by Linda Walsh Jenkins, published by the University of Minnesota Press in 1975.)

Each season's production schedule includes fantasies and adventures from the world's classic literature, rendered in original adaptations, along with new stories and plays written specifically for the company. The staff members take part in the selection of the plays, and the students in the theater school are encouraged to offer their suggestions. The company uses the following general criteria in choosing scripts for a season's productions: Does the group of scripts offer variety and balance in style, historical periods, and content? Are there stories for the very young as well as for teenagers? Do the stories, plays, and themes complement school curricula? Are the scripts exciting to the director, actors, designer, and composer who will join forces to produce them?

The shows in the company's complete repertoire for a given season (including workshops and adult plays) vary widely in style and approach. For example, the 1971–72 season began with Timothy Mason's *Robin Hood* in a naturalistic forest setting, which gave way six weeks later to Richard Shaw's Kabuki version of *Sleeping Beauty*. These were followed by a pair of plays: John Jenkins's *Hansel and Gretel* in the daytime opposite a stylish rendition of Richard Brinsley Sheridan's *The School for Scandal* in the evening. The final major offerings of the season were John Donahue's *The Cookie Jar* and his premiere play version of Ludwig Bemelmans's *Madeline and the Gypsies*. Concurrently with the main season, however, Le Petit Théâtre (a workshop series of adult productions initiated by the staff) presented *Spoon River Anthology* (an arrangement by director John Jenkins, based on the original poems), *The Sitwells at Sea* (a montage of images and poetry scripted by Donahue and Gar Hildenbrand), *Variations on a Similar Theme — An Homage to René Magritte* (a group of short surrealistic plays by Donahue), and *An Evening of Leonard Cohen* (poetry and songs arranged and directed by Hiram Titus). At the end of the season the company prepared Donahue's *Hang On to Your Head* and *Potpourri* (a performance-demonstration of the company's work with teenagers) for the ASSITEJ conventions in Montreal and Albany and for subsequent engagements on the East Coast.

The plays in this volume reflect the emerging vitality of the Children's Theatre Company during its first decade. The move into the new theater facility in 1974 plunged the company into a new world of practical and artistic challenges, and it remains to be seen how the new environment and circumstances will affect the structure and content of the company's productions in the years to come. The children's plays in this volume serve as models representing a standard of excellence that will continue to challenge the creative life and work of the Children's Theatre Company in the future.

Linda Walsh Jenkins

Five Plays from the Children's Theatre
Company of Minneapolis

About the Plays

The five adaptations of classic tales that appear in this volume were written expressly for the Children's Theatre Company of the Minneapolis Society of Fine Arts, its stage and technical facilities, and the talents of its resident acting personnel. The stage directions in the scripts reflect the way the plays were directed and performed by the company; although the stage directions may help the reader to visualize the plays and to become aware of the company's production methods, the company encourages other groups to develop their own interpretations of the scripts. The staging requirements are such that most of the plays can be produced by both professional and amateur groups, and the fact that many of the roles were written to be performed by teenagers makes the plays suitable for high school drama students. The photographs of scenes from productions of the plays and the excerpts from the scores of *A Christmas Carol, The Legend of Sleepy Hollow*, and *Robin Hood: A Story of the Forest* are included to suggest further the color and the atmosphere that were evoked in the productions. (The lyrics in the scripts are footnoted to indicate the pages on which the music appears.)

As in all plays developed by the Children's Theatre Company, the dynamic interaction among all the people involved in the productions had much to do with the final script versions published in this book. Each of the playwrights collaborated with the staff throughout the development of his script, often making changes in the final days before the opening of the show. Frederick Gaines, who wrote the adaptations of *A Christmas Carol* and *The Legend of Sleepy Hollow* (both of which were first directed by the company's artistic director, John Clark

3

Donahue), describes his relationship to Donahue and the company, their effect on his work, and his role as playwright:

John and I never worked together in the sense of polishing a play. There were no story sessions, no criticism, no questions asking for elaboration or change. John and I share a language of images. John always talked of being a "playmaker" rather than a "writer of plays," and I think I became a playmaker with him. Too much time is devoted to the *playwright's* vision. . . . I don't think that playwrights are prophets, but I hope that they are accurate and that they have access to their emotions. I think that the techniques a writer uses aren't much different from those a sculptor might use.

In John's theater I had access for the first time to the materials of theater — the designer, the composer, the actor. I don't mean that they were there in rehearsal — they were there long before the rehearsals began. The large production meetings shaped the whole of the play for me, and all that I really had to do was listen, remember, and edit. I listened to Jack Barkla [the designer] talk about the feel and the look of the play — specific things, not personal commentary — and then I listened to Roberta Carlson [the composer] and John talk about the sound of a play, the rhythms of a play.

Too often writers and directors feel that they must just be themselves, express themselves in their productions, and the uniqueness of the production will carry it. That's nonsense. When we met to talk about plays, we constantly spoke about the play in terms that revealed our debts. We talked about creating a setting like Rackham's illustrations; we talked of creating a specific moment onstage like that created by a particular ballerina in a particular performance; we talked of music that would evoke in the audience (as it did in us) the memory of childhood carols. These are borrowings. Not plagiarisms, but borrowings. We took the image of other works and let them work through us, let them reemerge in a coloring that was our own. That's the only way theater can work. If any part of the theater machine becomes selfish, a vehicle for personal dictatorship, then I think the theater is hurt by it. John's theater is the first theater democracy I've ever worked in. Theater must be a sharing of ideas or it becomes presumptuous.

Timothy Mason, whose two plays for the company were written and produced after Gaines's plays, received the 1972 National Society of Arts and Letters Award for *Kidnapped in London*, which he wrote while he was a sophomore in college. While still in high school, Mason had acted in numerous plays at the Children's Theatre Company, and the experience with the company had stimulated his interest in playwriting. He discusses the personal significance the play had for him and for many members of the company who worked on the production under the direction of John Donahue:

From the age of fifteen I was virtually raised in and by a professional company of adult and child actors . . . as was the young protagonist of *Kidnapped in London*. Thus, on one level, the play speaks for myself and my "fellow prisoners" in the exciting and sometimes harsh world of theater. However, any interest which the play may hold is not limited to some elite circle of child-actors. My years of experience working with and for children (and of course my own childhood) have taught me that there is no creature more full of *yearning* than a young girl or boy. The gestures of childhood seem to be a reaching, grasping, sometimes almost envious striving for a world which lies waiting. For an audience of children life on the stage becomes a metaphor for all of the yearnings that spell out the meaning of childhood.

Mason developed his second play, *Robin Hood: A Story of the Forest*, together with Bain Boehlke, who directed the show and played the role of Will Scarlet. The production was controversial because the script's approach to the Robin Hood story is different from popular versions, especially the film animations and the television series which some members of the audience remembered. Some adults found it upsetting to be reminded that Robin Hood's people were long-haired outlaws who followed a communal life-style in the forest. In a staff discussion of the play's origins, successes, and difficulties, Mason, Boehlke, and Donahue talked about the kinds of problems they had encountered in choosing themes and subjects for the play that would be suitable for children's theater.

MASON. People have said, "It's not what I expected!" Of course it isn't! It wasn't by chance that I wrote this type of story. To begin with, I had only the name of Robin Hood: "Write a play about Robin Hood." Then the nature of the legends about Robin Hood had some bearing on the choices I had to make. Reading the legends, I found that they are simple, pure adventure stories; individual characters are types, characterization is minimal, and plot is everything. And, because we are most familiar with a romantic nineteenth-century version of Robin Hood, our memory of the flavor of the stories is romantic. Since the legends are adventure stories, they are arranged in episodic style in which each story is a unit and is complete in itself. One might take just one of those adventure stories and make a play out of it, or one might take several of the stories and lay them out episodically with a build to one remarkable story at the end. I chose not to do that, since I was more interested in examining the life-style of the people in the forest than in telling an adventure story.

BOEHLKE. Instead of portraying a character in danger, we wanted to portray the *quality* of danger. Their life in the forest wasn't idyllic, by any means. It was, perhaps, in the beginning, but winter comes to the forest.

Mason chose to develop the conflict within the outlaw band rather than to rely solely on the format of the adventure episodes in which forces from outside, like the Sheriff, threaten the band. He invented a malcontent Will Scarlet, who is a surprising figure to encounter in young people's theater — Scarlet drinks, for fear of the winter and the struggle.

DONAHUE. As you know, these extra dimensions are not typical of most plays done for young people. Yet if you ask intelligent, creative people to become involved in writing for the young, I think that you have to expect dimensions, depth, and handling of the subject matter that go beyond what people have come to expect.

MASON. Why should audiences fear Will Scarlet when children and adults can tour an art museum and encounter scenes of actual violence without being upset? I've seen children standing in front of Scipio Atticus defeating Hannibal, with heads going off . . .

DONAHUE. Theater heightens the situation by a reenactment in a ritualized way of certain events by the priests who represent the people, and consequently it is more awful in its impact than the rattle or the cross or the drawing in the sand or the chanting because you actually see the hand coming down and the knife, or you see the head flying and you hear the voices. And consequently the theater is more difficult for the audience to come to and the violence more real than it is in the painting.

Mason noted that the children in the audience seemed relatively inattentive during the banquet scene in *Robin Hood* but that he recalled a scene involving no real "action" in Donahue's *How Could You Tell?* In that scene, "On the Wharf in the Night Rain," the audience was very attentive to a long series of speeches.

DONAHUE. The scene had to do with being about to set off on a perilous journey — after the house had burned down. If during the banquet scene in *Robin Hood* someone had been bringing in more and more of something, garlands or whatever, so that there was a parallel activity describing the interior activity, the children would understand. These things are very important. . . . In the scene where Will Scarlet and Robin Hood are circling one another, the physical ritual is one of pushing and shoving, punch and tackle. It is an extension of what kids do when they fight. It is a physical conflict which is very bold and basic, and the dialogue during that scene is abstract but significant in terms of the relationship between Will and Robin. The audience was very quiet and attentive during that scene. I'm convinced that if the dialogue had been delivered while Will and Robin were sitting on the log the children in the audience would have lost interest, but because it was delivered in juxtaposition with a physical exchange which the children know very well, they listened to the language. You know how they perceive; they have a profound intuitive understanding, and it manifests itself in ancient, primitive rites and behaviors — the piling of stones, the drawing of circles, the putting on of wooden wings, many things . . .

BOEHLKE. I don't think that is peculiar to children — that is what theater is.

DONAHUE. That is what we are talking about. And if we believe that certain things can be taught to children early and in ways that would have a profound effect on their souls, then you have a reason for being in the business we are in. You know, if we have any wisdom and skill as teachers and as artists, any visions that will illuminate, then it behooves us to invite the children in to share.

The third playwright represented in this volume, Richard Shaw, a poet, wrote *Sleeping Beauty* in cooperation with costume designer and director Gene Buck. Buck chose the Kabuki style as the vehicle for the production because he believed the style would be particularly well suited to the capabilities of the Children's Theatre Company; the term "ka-bu-ki" can be roughly translated as "singing-dancing-acting" and thus implies a combination of the very elements that are typically found in the company's plays. Shaw had acquired firsthand experience with authentic Kabuki theater during a period he had spent in Japan some years earlier. Most of the details in costuming and scenery were developed by Buck and set designer Jack Barkla from ideas suggested by descriptions and photographs of Kabuki and Japanese No plays. The production also borrowed from the Chinese film *A Night at the Peking Opera*, which provided inspiration for scenes such as the comic pantomime between the Prince and the boatman.

From the beginning the play was intended to be understood as a Western interpretation of an Oriental style. That is, the music is based on Japanese folk songs rendered in Western orchestration, and Kabuki conventions (such as the black-garbed prop men who change scenery and costumes in full view of the audience) and symbols of various kinds are included, but the play as a whole is given a Western frame by the Victorian parlor, the narrative format, and the Christmas carols.

Sleeping Beauty is an example of a play that came into being as a result of a Rockefeller Foundation subsidy that enabled the Children's Theatre Company to invite guest artists to participate in its productions. In awarding the grant the Foundation expressed the hope that the company would use part of the funds to encourage talented poets to become involved in writing works for children's theater. The Children's Theatre Company selected Richard Shaw, and the production of *Sleeping Beauty* was not only his first play but his first experience in working with a theater company: "At first I'd expected it to be a very simple job. It turned out to be far more complex. Initially I was even a little suspicious of this place. Then I discovered how well, how hard the company works. I found working with time limits sometimes very troublesome. For instance, there was the time I brought in what I thought were the roughs for some music and, before I had a chance to revise them, Roberta Carlson [the composer] already had them scored!''

Early in the "idea" stage of the script Buck asked Shaw to choose an image for Beauty that would run through the entire play. Shaw decided to use the image of a flower, and from this central image he developed the blessings ("May your sleep have the art of the morning glory . . ."), the implicit theme of Beauty "blooming" into young womanhood, and the metaphor of flowers killed by frost to signify the winter-death-sleep that overcomes Beauty and the entire kingdom. This poetic device was also carried out concretely in the design of the play (for example, the baby princess sleeps in a flower cradle).

In a sense Shaw wrote *Sleeping Beauty* for his own children and with their help, somewhat in the way that Grandfather in the play invents his narrative for Ben and Susan, who, like Shaw's children, enter into the story and take an active part in its development. When the contours of the play had begun to emerge, Shaw told the story to his children, who provided the point of view of the young theatergoers who would be the ultimate critics. From their perception of the play they were able to help Shaw detect minor flaws in the logic of events and characterization and to suggest improvements in the plot and in individual characters. For example, they wondered how the Ogress escaped the sleep that numbed the kingdom. Momentarily at a loss for an explanation, Shaw decided that the Ogress must transform herself into a spider that drowses briefly but awakens to spin its webs; in this way the theatrically effective Ogress/spider was engendered. The participation of the Shaw children illustrates another dimension of the interaction among people — playwrights, staff personnel, and others — that is inherent in all of the plays produced by the Children's Theatre Company.

Although productions are designed to please and intrigue audiences, there is inevitably a degree of tension between an audience's preconception of how a story should look and sound (frequently based on popular book illustrations, movies, or animated cartoons) and the choices made by artists of the theater. In the course of a staff discussion Donahue summed up what may be the greatest single difficulty in writing and producing good plays for children:

A play for children can last for only an hour and fifteen or twenty minutes, and yet it wants to deal with tales and myths that are enormous in their scope — and then it needs to be put on by people who are creative, artistic, and intelligent. Do you give the story a superficial treatment that deals with the main literary highlights, so that the kids report, "We saw his arrow, we saw Little John's staff, we saw Will Scarlet's red hair, we saw Friar Tuck, we saw Maid Marion (she was pretty with flowers in her hair), we saw the Sheriff (he was mean-looking), and then we went home . . ."? Or do we take one episode or one kind of idea or event and flesh it out? You know that this is a very important problem. This is what we are trying to get at and what the Rockefeller Foundation would like us to discover — how to do good plays for young people, plays that are exciting, that have some narrative literature, that attract the artist, that make the artist want to become deeply involved, and that are artistically rewarding.

The five plays that appear in print for the first time in this volume are examples of five very different solutions to the problems of artistically and dramatically rendering classic literature for children in theatrical forms. The arrangement of the plays in the book follows the chronological sequence in which they were first produced. When the five plays are considered in this order, the influence on the later plays of budget increases and various outside grants becomes apparent in the company's use of more elaborate settings in these plays and in its experimentation with nontraditional modes of storytelling in *Robin Hood* and *Sleeping Beauty*. Nevertheless, each of the five plays, the last no more than the first, reflects the general standards of artistic quality which the Children's Theatre Company has sought to attain throughout its history.

A Christmas Carol

Adapted by Frederick Gaines

SECOND SPIRIT
> *You are not the judge. Do not judge, then. It*
> *may be that in the sight of heaven you are more worthless*
> *and less fit to live than millions like this poor man's*
> *child. Oh God! To hear an insect on a leaf pronouncing*
> *that there is too much life among his hungry brothers in the dust.*

This adaptation of Charles Dickens's *A Christmas Carol* was first produced by the Children's Theatre Company of the Minneapolis Society of Fine Arts in November 1968. The script was edited by Linda Walsh Jenkins with the assistance of Carol K. Metz.

Cast of Characters

Carolers, families, dancers
First boy
Second boy
Third boy
Little girl with a doll
Ebenezer Scrooge
Fred, Scrooge's nephew
Bob Cratchit, Scrooge's clerk
Gentleman visitor
Warder and residents of the poorhouse
Sparsit, Scrooge's servant
Cook
Charwoman
Jacob Marley
Leper
First spirit (the Spirit of Christmas Past)
Jack Walton

Ben Benjamin
Child Scrooge
Fan, Scrooge's sister
Fezziwig
Dick Wilkins
Young Ebenezer
Sweetheart of Young Ebenezer
Second spirit (the Spirit of Christmas Present)
Mrs. Cratchit
Several Cratchit children
Tiny Tim
Hunger and Ignorance, the beggar children
Pawnbroker
Third spirit (the Spirit of Christmas Yet to Come)
Butcher
Coachman

Sequence of Scenes

Overture   "Christ the King, My Gentle One"
Scene i   Scrooge in His Shop
Scene ii   Scrooge Goes Home
Scene iii   The Spirit of Christmas Past
Scene iv   The Spirit of Christmas Present
Scene v   The Spirit of Christmas Yet to Come
Scene vi   Scrooge's Conversion

Notes on the Play

Ebenezer Scrooge, obsessed with solitude and greed, collides in a nightmare with his own youth and his lost love. In Frederick Gaines's theatrical adaptation of Charles Dickens's story, Scrooge is visited by the spirits of Christmas Past, Christmas Present, and Christmas Yet to Come in scenes that flow rapidly from one to the next, activated by images from memory that appear suddenly and instantly transform the setting. Carolers sing fragments of joyous Christmas songs in the corners of Scrooge's mind, and a little girl with a doll accompanies him on the street and joins him on his dream-journey. The visiting spirits of Christmas force Scrooge to confront people and scenes from his life that remind him of his friendlessness — he even sees his home and his future corpse being rifled by his own servants. Finally, he awakens to the reality of Christmas morning and discovers the joy of giving, loving, and caring for others.

The play is designed to be produced in a simply mounted, nonrealistic setting. A high platform that serves as Scrooge's bed is at downstage right. The space under it forms the entrance to Scrooge's office. A series of stairs and ramps makes a curving sweep from the bed across the upstage area and slopes down to a chair-high platform at left center. The set is painted black and is hung with dark textured fabrics at the back and the sides. The props include candles, lanterns, the little girl's doll, and platters of food and bowls of drink for Fezziwig's party. The set furnishings include Scrooge's writing desk, the Cratchits' armchair, and chandeliers for the parties. The costumes, based on fashions of nineteenth-century London, provide color and texture against the abstract setting.

13

Overture   "Christ the King,
My Gentle One"

The play begins amid a swirl of street life in Victorian London. Happy groups pass; brightly costumed carolers and families call out to one another and sing "Joy to the World." Three boys and a girl are grouped about a glowing mound of coal. As the carolers leave the stage, the lights dim and the focus shifts to the mound of coals, bright against the dark. Slowly, the children begin to respond to the warmth. A piano plays softly as the children talk.

FIRST BOY

I saw a horse in a window. (*pause*) A dapple . . . gray and white. And a saddle, too . . . red. And a strawberry mane down to here. All new. Golden stirrups. (*People pass by the children, muttering greetings to one another.*)

SECOND BOY

Christmas Eve.

THIRD BOY

Wish we could go.

FIRST BOY

So do I.

THIRD BOY

I think I'd like it.

FIRST BOY

Oh, wouldn't I . . . wouldn't I!

14

SECOND BOY

> We're going up onto the roof. (*The boys look at him quizzically.*) My father's a glass. Telescope. A brass one. It opens up and it has twists on it and an eyepiece that you put up to look through. We can see all the way to the park with it.

THIRD BOY

> Could I look through it?

SECOND BOY

> Maybe . . . where would you look? (*The third boy points straight up.*) Why there?

THIRD BOY

> I'd like to see the moon. (*The boys stand and look upward as the girl sings to her doll. One of the boys makes a snow angel on the ground.*)

GIRL

> (*singing*)
>
>> *Christ the King came down one day,*
>> *Into this world of ours,*
>> *And crying from a manger bed,*
>> *Began the Christmas hour.*
>
> (*speaking*)
>
>> *Christ the King, my pretty one,*
>> *Sleep softly on my breast.*
>> *Christ the King, my gentle one,*
>> *Show us the way to rest.*
>
> (*She begins to sing the first verse again. As snow starts to fall on the boy making the snow angel, he stands up and reaches out to catch a single flake.*)

Scene i   Scrooge in His Shop

The percussion thunders. Scrooge hurls himself through the descending snowflakes and sends the children scattering. They retreat, watching. Cratchit comes in. He takes some coal from the mound and puts it into a small bucket; as he carries it to a corner of the stage, the stage area is transformed from street to office. Scrooge's nephew Fred enters, talks with the children, gives them coins, and sends them away with a "Merry Christmas."

FRED

A Merry Christmas, Uncle! God save you!

SCROOGE

Bah! Humbug!

FRED

Christmas a humbug, Uncle? I hope that's meant as a joke.

SCROOGE

Well, it's not. Come, come, what is it you want? Don't waste all the day, Nephew.

FRED

I want only to wish you a Merry Christmas, Uncle. Don't be cross.

SCROOGE

What else can I be when I live in such a world of fools as this? Merry Christmas! Out with Merry Christmas! What's Christmas to you but a time for paying bills without money; a time for finding yourself a year older and not an hour richer. If I could work my will, every idiot who goes about with "Merry Christmas" on his lips should be boiled with his own pudding and buried with a stake of holly through his heart.

FRED

Uncle!

SCROOGE

Nephew, keep Christmas in your own way and let me keep it in mine.

FRED

But you don't keep it.

SCROOGE

Let me leave it alone then. Much good may it do you. Much good it has ever done you.

FRED

There are many things from which I might have derived good by which I have not profited, I daresay, Christmas among the rest. And though it has never put a scrap of gold in my pocket, I believe it has done me good and will do me good, and I say, God bless it!

SCROOGE

Bah!

FRED

Don't be angry, Uncle. Come! Dine with us tomorrow.

SCROOGE

I'll dine alone, thank you.

FRED

But why?

SCROOGE

Why? Why did you get married?

FRED

Why, because I fell in love with a wonderful girl.

SCROOGE

And I with solitude. Good afternoon.

FRED

Nay, Uncle, but you never came to see me before I was married. Why give it as a reason for not coming now?

SCROOGE

Good afternoon.

FRED

I am sorry with all my heart to find you so determined; but I have made the attempt in homage to Christmas, and I'll keep that good spirit to the last. So, a Merry Christmas, Uncle.

SCROOGE

Good afternoon!

FRED

And a Happy New Year!

SCROOGE

Good afternoon! (*Fred hesitates as if to say something more. He sees that Scrooge has gone to get a volume down from the shelf, and so he starts to leave. As he leaves, the doorbell rings.*) Bells. Is it necessary to always have bells? (*The gentleman visitor enters, causing the doorbell to ring again.*) Cratchit!

CRATCHIT

Yes, sir?

SCROOGE

The bell, fool! See to it!

CRATCHIT

Yes, sir. (*He goes to the entrance.*)

SCROOGE

(*muttering*) Merry Christmas . . . Wolves howling and a Merry Christmas . . .

CRATCHIT

It's for you, sir.

SCROOGE

Of course it's for me. You're not receiving callers, are you? Show them in.

CRATCHIT

Right this way, sir. (*The gentleman visitor approaches Scrooge.*)

SCROOGE

Yes, yes?

GENTLEMAN VISITOR

Scrooge and Marley's, I believe. Have I the pleasure of addressing Mr. Scrooge or Mr. Marley?

SCROOGE

Marley's dead. Seven years tonight. What is it you want?

GENTLEMAN VISITOR

I have no doubt that his liberality is well represented by his surviving partner. Here, sir, my card. (*He hands Scrooge his business card.*)

SCROOGE

Liberality? No doubt of it? All right, all right, I can read. What is it you want? (*He returns to his work.*)

GENTLEMAN VISITOR

At this festive season of the year . . .

SCROOGE

It's winter and cold. (*He continues his work and ignores the gentleman visitor.*)

GENTLEMAN VISITOR

Yes . . . yes, it is, and the more reason for my visit. At this time of the year it is more than usually desirable to make some slight provision for the poor and destitute who suffer greatly from the cold. Many thousands are in want of common necessaries; hundreds of thousands are in want of common comforts, sir.

SCROOGE

Are there no prisons?

GENTLEMAN VISITOR

Many, sir.

SCROOGE

And the workhouse? Is it still in operation?

GENTLEMAN VISITOR

It is, still, I wish I could say it was not.

SCROOGE

The poor law is still in full vigor then?

GENTLEMAN VISITOR

Yes, sir.

SCROOGE

I'm glad to hear it. From what you said, I was afraid someone had stopped its operation.

GENTLEMAN VISITOR

Under the impression that they scarcely furnish Christian cheer of mind or body to the multitude, a few of us are endeavoring to raise a fund to buy the poor some meat and drink and means of warmth. We choose this time because it is the time, of all others, when want is keenly felt and abundance rejoices. May I put you down for something, sir?

SCROOGE

(*retreating into the darkness temporarily*) Nothing.

GENTLEMAN VISITOR

You wish to be anonymous?

SCROOGE

I wish to be left alone. Since you ask me what I wish, sir, that is my answer. I don't make merry myself at Christmas and I can't afford to make idle people merry. I help support the establishments I have mentioned . . . they cost enough . . . and those who are poorly off must go there.

GENTLEMAN VISITOR

Many can't go there, and many would rather die.

SCROOGE

If they would rather die, they had better do it and decrease the surplus population. That is not my affair. My business is. It occupies me constantly. (*He talks both to the gentleman visitor and to himself while he thumbs through his books.*) Ask a man to give up life and means . . . fine thing. What is it, I want to know? Charity? Damned charity! (*His nose deep in his books, he vaguely hears the dinner bell being rung in the workhouse; he looks up as if he has heard it but never focuses on the actual scene. The warder of the poorhouse stands in a pool of light at the far left, slowly ringing a bell.*)

WARDER

Dinner. All right. Line up. (*The poorly clad, dirty residents of the poorhouse line up and file by to get their evening dish of gruel, wordlessly accepting it and going back to eat listlessly in the gloom. Scrooge returns to the business of his office. The procession continues for a moment, then the image of the poorhouse is obscured by darkness. The dejected gentleman visitor exits.*)

SCROOGE

Latch the door, Cratchit. Firmly, firmly. Draft as cold as Christmas blowing in here. Charity! (*Cratchit goes to the door, starts to close it, then sees the little girl with the doll. She seems to beckon to him; he moves slowly toward her, and they dance together for a moment. Scrooge continues to work. Suddenly carolers appear on the platform, and a few phrases of their carol, "Angels We Have Heard on High," are heard. Scrooge looks up.*) Cratchit! (*As soon as Scrooge shouts, the girl and the carolers vanish and Cratchit begins to close up the shop.*) Cratchit!

CRATCHIT

Yes, sir.

SCROOGE

Well, to work then!

CRATCHIT

It's evening, sir.

SCROOGE

Is it?

CRATCHIT

Christmas evening, sir.

SCROOGE

Oh, you'll want all day tomorrow off, I suppose.

CRATCHIT

If it's quite convenient, sir.

SCROOGE

It's not convenient, and it's not fair. If I was to deduct half a crown from your salary for it, you'd think yourself ill used, wouldn't you? Still you expect me to pay a day's wage for a day of no work.

CRATCHIT

It's only once a year, sir.

SCROOGE

Be here all the earlier the next morning.

CRATCHIT

I will, sir.

SCROOGE

Then off, off.

CRATCHIT

Yes, sir! Merry Christmas, sir!

SCROOGE

Bah! (*As soon as Cratchit opens the door, the sounds of the street begin, very bright and loud. Cratchit is caught up in a swell of people hurrying through the street. Children pull him along to the top of an ice slide, and he runs and slides down it, disappearing in darkness as the stage suddenly is left almost empty. Scrooge goes around the room blowing out the candles, talking to himself.*) Christmas Eve. Carolers! Bah! There. Another day. (*He opens his door and peers out.*) Black, very black. Now where are they? (*The children are heard singing carols for a moment.*) Begging pennies for their songs, are they? Oh, boy! Here, boy! (*The little girl emerges from the shadows. Scrooge hands her a dark lantern and she holds it while he lights it with an ember from the pile of coals.*)

Scene ii   Scrooge Goes Home

SCROOGE

(*talking to the little girl*) Hold it quiet! There. Off now. That's it. High. Black as pitch. Light the street, that's it. You're a bright lad! Good to see that. Earn your supper, boy. You'll not go hungry this night. Home. You know the way, do you? Yes, that's the way. The house of Ebenezer Scrooge. (*As the two find their way to Scrooge's house, the audience sees and hears a brief image of a cathedral interior with a living crèche and a large choir singing "Amen!"; the image ends in a blackout. The lights come up immediately, and Scrooge is at his door.*) Hold the light up, boy, up. (*The girl with the lantern disappears.*) Where did he go? Boy? No matter. There's a penny saved. Lantern's gone out. No matter. A candle saved. Yes, here's the key. (*He turns with the key toward the door, and Marley's face swims out of the darkness. Scrooge watches, unable to speak. He fumbles for a match, lights the lantern, and swings it toward the figure, which melts away. Pause. Scrooge fits the key in the lock and turns it as the door suddenly is opened from the inside by the porter, Sparsit. Scrooge is startled, then recovers.*) Sparsit?

SPARSIT

Yes, sir?

SCROOGE

Hurry, hurry. The door . . . close it.

SPARSIT

Did you knock, sir?

SCROOGE

Knock? What matter? Here, light me up the stairs.

SPARSIT

Yes, sir. (*He leads Scrooge up the stairs. They pass the cook on the way. Scrooge brushes by her, stops, looks back, and she leans toward him.*)

COOK

Something to warm you, sir? Porridge?

SCROOGE

Wha . . . ? No. No, nothing.

COOK

(*waiting for her Christmas coin*) Merry Christmas, sir. (*Scrooge ignores the request and the cook disappears. Mumbling, Scrooge follows Sparsit.*)

SCROOGE

(*looking back after the cook is gone*) Fright a man nearly out of his life . . . Merry Christmas . . . bah!

SPARSIT

Your room, sir.

SCROOGE

Hmmm? Oh, yes, yes. And good night.

SPARSIT

(*extending his hand for his coin*) Merry Christmas, sir.

SCROOGE

Yes, yes . . . (*He sees the outstretched hand; he knows what Sparsit wants and is infuriated.*) Out! Out! (*He closes the door after Sparsit, turns toward his chamber, and discovers the charwoman directly behind him.*)

CHARWOMAN

Warm your bed for you, sir?

SCROOGE

What? Out! Out!

CHARWOMAN

Aye, sir. (*She starts for the door. Marley's voice is heard mumbling something unintelligible.*)

SCROOGE

What's that?

CHARWOMAN

Me, sir? Not a thing, sir.

SCROOGE

Then, good night.

CHARWOMAN

Good night. (*She exits and Scrooge pantomimes shutting the door behind her. The voice of Marley over an offstage microphone whispers and reverberates: "Merry Christmas, Scrooge!" Silence. Scrooge hears the voice but cannot account for it. He climbs up to open a window and looks down. A cathedral choir singing "O Come, All Ye Faithful" is heard in the distance. Scrooge listens a moment, shuts the window, and prepares for bed. As soon as he has shut the sound out of his room, figures appear; they seem to be coming down the main aisle of a church, bearing gifts to the living crèche. The orchestra plays "O Come, All Ye Faithful" as the procession files out. Scrooge, ready for bed, warms himself before the heap of coals. As he pulls his nightcap from a chair, a small handbell tumbles off onto the floor. Startled, he picks it up and rings it for reassurance; an echo answers it. He turns and sees*)

*the little girl on the street; she is swinging her doll, which pro-
duces the echo of his bell. Scrooge escapes to his bed; the girl is
swallowed up in the darkness. The bell sounds grow to a din,
incoherent as in a dream, then suddenly fall silent. Scrooge sits up
in bed, listens, and hears the chains of Marley coming up the
stairs. Scrooge reaches for the bellpull to summon Sparsit. The
bell responds with a gong, and Marley appears. He and Scrooge
face one another.)*

SCROOGE

What do you want with me?

MARLEY

(*in a ghostly, unreal voice*) Much.

SCROOGE

Who are you?

MARLEY

Ask who I was.

SCROOGE

Who were you?

MARLEY

In life, I was your partner, Jacob Marley.

SCROOGE

He's dead.

MARLEY

Seven years this night, Ebenezer Scrooge.

SCROOGE

Why do you come here?

MARLEY

I must. It is commanded me. I must wander the world and see what
I can no longer share, what I would not share when I walked where
you do.

SCROOGE

And must go thus?

MARLEY

The chain? Look at it, Ebenezer, study it. Locks and vaults and
golden coins. I forged it, each link, each day when I sat in these

chairs, commanded these rooms. Greed, Ebenezer Scrooge, wealth. Feel them, know them. Yours was as heavy as this I wear seven years ago and you have labored to build it since.

SCROOGE

If you're here to lecture, I have no time for it. It is late, the night is cold. I want comfort now.

MARLEY

I have none to give. I know not how you see me this night. I did not ask it. I have sat invisible beside you many and many a day. I am commanded to bring you a chance, Ebenezer. Heed it!

SCROOGE

Quickly then, quickly.

MARLEY

You will be haunted by three spirits.

SCROOGE

(*scoffing*) Is that the chance?

MARLEY

Mark it.

SCROOGE

I do not choose to.

MARLEY

(*ominously*) Then you will walk where I do, burdened by your riches, your greed.

SCROOGE

Spirits mean nothing to me.

MARLEY

(*slowly leaving*) Expect the first tomorrow, when the bell tolls one, the second on the next night at the same hour, the third upon the next night when the last stroke of twelve has ended. Look to see me no more. I must wander. Look that, for your own sake, you remember what has passed between us.

SCROOGE

Jacob . . . Don't leave me! . . . Jacob! Jacob!

MARLEY

Adieu, Ebenezer. (*At Marley's last words a funeral procession begins to move across the stage. A boy walks in front; a priest follows, swinging a censer; sounds of mourning and the suggestion of church music are heard. Scrooge calls out, "Jacob, don't leave me!" as if talking in the midst of a bad dream. At the end of the procession is the little girl, swinging her doll and singing softly.)*

GIRL

> *Hushabye, don't you cry,*
> *Go to sleep, little baby.*
> *When you wake, you shall have*
> *All the pretty little horses,*
> *Blacks and bays, dapples and grays,*
> *All the pretty little horses.*

(She stops singing and looks up at Scrooge; their eyes meet and she solemnly rings the doll in greeting. Scrooge pulls shut the bed curtains and the girl exits. The bell sounds are picked up by the bells of a leper who enters, dragging himself along.)

LEPER

(calling out) Leper! Leper! Stay the way! Leper! Leper! Keep away! *(He exits and the clock begins to chime, ringing the hours. Scrooge sits up in bed and begins to count the chimes.)*

SCROOGE

Eight . . . nine . . . ten . . . eleven . . . it can't be . . . twelve. Midnight? No. Not twelve. It can't be. I haven't slept the whole day through. Twelve? Yes, yes, twelve noon. *(He hurries to the window and looks out.)* Black. Twelve midnight. *(pause)* I must get up. A day wasted. I must get down to the office. *(Two small chimes are heard.)* Quarter past. But it just rang twelve. Fifteen minutes haven't gone past, not so quickly. *(Again two small chimes are heard.)* A quarter to one. The spirit . . . It's to come at one. *(He hurries to his bed as the chimes ring again.)* One.

Scene iii   The Spirit of Christmas Past

The hour is struck again by a large street clock and the first spirit appears. It is a figure dressed to look like the little girl's doll.

SCROOGE

Are you the spirit whose coming was foretold to me?

FIRST SPIRIT

I am.

SCROOGE

Who and what are you?

FIRST SPIRIT

I am the Ghost of Christmas Past.

SCROOGE

Long past?

FIRST SPIRIT

Your past.

SCROOGE

Why are you here?

FIRST SPIRIT

Your welfare. Rise. Walk with me.

SCROOGE

I am mortal still. I cannot pass through air.

FIRST SPIRIT

My hand. (*Scrooge grasps the spirit's hand tightly, and the doll's bell rings softly. Scrooge remembers a scene from his past in which two boys greet each other in the street.*)

FIRST VOICE

Halloo, Jack!

SECOND VOICE

    Ben! Merry Christmas, Ben!

SCROOGE

    Jack Walton. Young Jack Walton. Spirits . . . ?

FIRST VOICE

    Have a good holiday, Jack.

SCROOGE

    Yes, yes, I remember him. Both of them. Little Ben Benjamin. He used to . . .

FIRST VOICE

    See you next term, Jack. Next . . . term . . .

SCROOGE

    They . . . they're off for the holidays and going home from school. It's Christmas time . . . all of the children off home now . . . No . . . no, not all . . . there was one . . . (*The spirit motions for Scrooge to turn, and he sees a young boy playing with a teddy bear and talking to it.*) Yes . . . reading . . . poor boy.

FIRST SPIRIT

    What, I wonder?

SCROOGE

    Reading? Oh, it was nothing. Fancy, all fancy and make-believe and take-me-away. All of it. Yes, nonsense.

CHILD SCROOGE

    Ali Baba.

SCROOGE

    Yes . . . that was it.

CHILD SCROOGE

    Genii, take me to the Gate of Damascus.

SCROOGE

    Yes, O Master, and jewels I shall bring to you, and gold and myrrh and frankincense.

CHILD SCROOGE

    And they put him down — do you remember — that silly one, at the Gate of Damascus, in his underdrawers — asleep!

SCROOGE

> Yes, yes, the genii turned the Sultan's groom upside down and stood him on his head — served him right, I say!

CHILD SCROOGE

> And all the thieves and the jars of oil . . . (*Scrooge pretends to stab the jars with his scimitar.*)

SCROOGE

> Yes, yes, and running them through — this and this and this for each of you!

CHILD SCROOGE

> Yes, and remember . . . and remember . . . remember Robinson Crusoe?

SCROOGE

> And the parrot!

CHILD SCROOGE

> Yes, the parrot! I love him best.

SCROOGE

> (*imitating the parrot*) With his stripey green body and yellow tail drooping along and couldn't sing — awk — but could talk, and a thing like a lettuce growing out the top of his head . . . and he used to sit on the very top of the tree — up there.

CHILD SCROOGE

> And Robinson Crusoe sailed around the island and he thought he had escaped the island and the parrot said, the parrot said . . .

SCROOGE

> (*imitating the parrot*) Robinson Crusoe, where you been? Awk! Robinson Crusoe, where you been?

CHILD SCROOGE

> And Robinson Crusoe looked up in the tree and saw the parrot and knew he hadn't escaped and he was still there, still all alone there.

SCROOGE

> Poor Robinson Crusoe.

CHILD SCROOGE

> (*sadly replacing the teddy bear*) Poor Robinson Crusoe.

SCROOGE

> Poor child. Poor child.

FIRST SPIRIT

Why poor?

SCROOGE

Fancy . . . fancy . . . (*He tries to mask his feelings by being brusque.*) It's his way, a child's way to . . . to lose being alone in . . . in dreams, dreams . . . Never matter if they are all nonsense, yes, nonsense. But he'll be all right, grow out of it. Yes. Yes, he did outgrow it, the nonsense. Became a man and left there and he became, yes, he became a man and . . . yes, successful . . . rich! (*The sadness returns.*) Never matter . . . never matter. (*Fan runs in and goes to Child Scrooge.*) Fan!

FAN

Brother, dear brother! (*She kisses Child Scrooge.*)

CHILD SCROOGE

Dear, dear Fan.

FAN

I've come to bring you home, home for good and ever. Come with me, come now. (*She takes his hand and they start to run off, but the spirit stops them and signals for the light on them to fade. They look at the spirit, aware of their role in the spirit's "education" of Scrooge.*)

SCROOGE

Let me watch them go? Let them be happy for a moment! (*The spirit says nothing. Scrooge turns away from them and the light goes out.*) A delicate, delicate child. A breath might have withered her.

FIRST SPIRIT

She died a woman and had, as I remember, children.

SCROOGE

One child.

FIRST SPIRIT

Your nephew.

SCROOGE

Yes, yes, Fred, my nephew. (*Scrooge pauses, then tries to bluster through.*) Well? Well, all of us have that, haven't we? Child-hoods? Sadnesses? But we grow and we become men, masters of

ourselves. (*The spirit gestures for the music "Fezziwig's Party"* *
to begin. It is heard first as from a great distance, then Scrooge
becomes aware of it.) I've no time for it, Spirit. Music and all of
your Christmas falderol. Yes, yes, I've learnt what you have to
show me. (*Fezziwig, Young Ebenezer, and Dick appear, busily*
preparing for the party.)

FEZZIWIG

Yo ho, there! Ebenezer! Dick!

SCROOGE

Fezziwig! It's old Fezziwig that I 'prenticed under.

FIRST SPIRIT

Your master?

SCROOGE

Oh, aye, and the best that any boy could have. There's Dick
Wilkins! Bless me. He was very much attached to me was Dick.
Poor Dick. Dear, dear.

FEZZIWIG

Yo ho, my boys! No more work tonight. Christmas Eve, Dick!
Christmas, Ebenezer! Let's have the shutters up before a man can
say Jack Robinson! (*The music continues. Chandeliers are pulled*
into position, and mistletoe, holly, and ivy are draped over every-
thing by bustling servants. Dancers fill the stage for Fezziwig's
wonderful Christmas party. In the midst of the dancing and the
gaiety servants pass back and forth through the crowd with huge
platters of food. At a pause in the music, Young Ebenezer, who is
dancing, calls out.)

YOUNG EBENEZER

Mr. Fezziwig, sir, you're a wonderful master!

SCROOGE and YOUNG EBENEZER

A wonderful master!

SCROOGE

(*echoing the phrase*) A wonderful master! (*The music changes*
suddenly and the dancers jerk into distorted postures and then
begin to move in slow motion. The celebrants slowly exit, perform-
ing a macabre dance to discordant sounds.)

*Music on pages 52–55.

FIRST SPIRIT

Just because he gave a party? It was very small.

SCROOGE

Small!

FIRST SPIRIT

He spent a few pounds of your "mortal" money, three, four at the most. Is that so much that he deserves this praise?

SCROOGE

But it wasn't the money. He had the power to make us happy, to make our service light or burdensome. The happiness he gives is quite as great as if it cost a fortune. That's what . . . a good master is.

FIRST SPIRIT

Yes?

SCROOGE

No, no, nothing.

FIRST SPIRIT

Something, I think.

SCROOGE

I should like to be able to say a word or two to my clerk just now, that's all.

FIRST SPIRIT

But this is all past. Your clerk Cratchit couldn't be here.

SCROOGE

No, no, of course not, an idle thought. Are we done?

FIRST SPIRIT

(*motioning for the waltz music to begin*) Nearly.

SCROOGE

(*hearing the waltz and remembering it*) Surely it's enough. Haven't you tormented me enough? (*Young Ebenezer is seen waltzing with his sweetheart.*)

FIRST SPIRIT

I only show the past, what it promised you. Look. Another promise.

SCROOGE

Oh. Oh, yes. I had forgotten . . . her. Don't they dance beautifully? So young, so young. I would have married her if only . . .

SWEETHEART

Can you love me, Ebenezer? I bring no dowry to my marriage, only me, only love. It is no currency that you can buy and sell with, but we can live with it. Can you? (*She pauses, then returns the ring Scrooge gave her as his pledge.*) I release you, Ebenezer, for the love of the man you once were. Will that man win me again, now that he is free?

SCROOGE

(*trying to speak to her*) If only you had held me to it. You should not have let me go. I was young, I did love you.

SWEETHEART

(*speaking to Young Ebenezer*) We have never lied to one another. May you be happy in the life you have chosen. Good-bye. (*She runs out. Young Ebenezer slowly leaves.*)

SCROOGE

No, no, it was not meant that way . . . !

FIRST SPIRIT

You cannot change now what you would not change then. I am your mistakes, Ebenezer Scrooge, all of the things you could have done and did not.

SCROOGE

Then leave me! I have done them. I shall live with them. As I have, as I do; as I will.

FIRST SPIRIT

There is another Christmas, seven years.ago, when Marley died.

SCROOGE

No! I will not see it. I will not! He died. I could not prevent it. I did not choose for him to die on Christmas Day.

FIRST SPIRIT

And when his day was chosen, what did you do then?

SCROOGE

I looked after his affairs.

FIRST SPIRIT

His business.

SCROOGE

Yes! His business! Mine! It was all that I had, all that I could do in this world. I have nothing to do with the world to come after.

FIRST SPIRIT

Then I will leave you.

SCROOGE

Not yet! Don't leave me here! Tell me what I must do! What of the other spirits?

FIRST SPIRIT

They will come.

SCROOGE

And you? What of you?

FIRST SPIRIT

I am always with you. (*The little girl appears with her doll; she takes Scrooge's hand and gently leads him to bed. Numbed, he follows her. She leans against the foot of the bed, ringing the doll and singing. The first spirit exits as she sings.*)

GIRL

> *When you wake, you shall have*
> *All the pretty little horses,*
> *Blacks and bays, dapples and grays,*
> *All the pretty little horses.*

(*She rings the doll and the ringing becomes the chiming of Scrooge's bell. The girl exits. Scrooge sits upright in bed as he hears the chimes.*)

SCROOGE

A minute until one. No one here. No one's coming. (*A larger clock strikes one o'clock.*)

Scene iv   The Spirit of Christmas Present

A light comes on. Scrooge becomes aware of it and goes slowly to it. He sees the second spirit, the Spirit of Christmas Present, who looks like Fezziwig.

SCROOGE
    Fezziwig!
SECOND SPIRIT
    Hello, Scrooge.
SCROOGE
    But you can't be . . . not Fezziwig.
SECOND SPIRIT
    Do you see me as him?
SCROOGE
    I do.
SECOND SPIRIT
    And hear me as him?
SCROOGE
    I do.
SECOND SPIRIT
    I wish I were the gentleman, so as not to disappoint you.
SCROOGE
    But you're not . . . ?
SECOND SPIRIT
    No, Mr. Scrooge. You have never seen the like of me before. I am the Ghost of Christmas Present.
SCROOGE
    But . . .

SECOND SPIRIT
> You see what you will see, Scrooge, no more. Will you walk out with me this Christmas Eve?

SCROOGE
> But I am not yet dressed.

SECOND SPIRIT
> Take my tails, dear boy, we're leaving.

SCROOGE
> Wait!

SECOND SPIRIT
> What is it now?

SCROOGE
> Christmas Present, did you say?

SECOND SPIRIT
> I did.

SCROOGE
> Then we are traveling here? In this town? London? Just down there?

SECOND SPIRIT
> Yes, yes, of course.

SCROOGE
> Then we could walk? Your flying is . . . well, too sudden for an old man. Well?

SECOND SPIRIT
> It's your Christmas, Scrooge; I am only the guide.

SCROOGE
> (*puzzled*) Then we can walk? (*The spirit nods.*) Where are you guiding me to?

SECOND SPIRIT
> Bob Cratchit's.

SCROOGE
> My clerk?

SECOND SPIRIT
> You did want to talk to him? (*Scrooge pauses, uncertain how to answer.*) Don't worry, Scrooge, you won't have to.

SCROOGE

(trying to change the subject, to cover his error) Shouldn't be much of a trip. With fifteen bob a week, how far off can it be?

SECOND SPIRIT

A world away, Scrooge, at least that far. *(Scrooge and the spirit start to step off a curb when a funeral procession enters with a child's coffin, followed by the poorhouse children, who are singing. Seated on top of the coffin is the little girl. She and Scrooge look at one another.)* That is the way to it, Scrooge. *(The procession follows the coffin offstage; Scrooge and the spirit exit after the procession. As they leave, the lights focus on Mrs. Cratchit and her children. Mrs. Cratchit sings as she puts Tiny Tim and the other children to bed, all in one bed. She pulls a dark blanket over them.)*

MRS. CRATCHIT

(singing)

> *When you wake, you shall have*
> *All the pretty little horses,*
> *Blacks and bays, dapples and grays,*
> *All the pretty little horses.*

To sleep now, all of you. Christmas tomorrow. *(She kisses them and goes to Bob Cratchit, who is by the hearth.)* How did our little Tiny Tim behave?

BOB CRATCHIT

As good as gold and better. He told me, coming home, that he hoped the people saw him in the church because he was a cripple and it might be pleasant to them to remember upon Christmas Day who made the lame to walk and the blind to see.

MRS. CRATCHIT

He's a good boy. *(The second spirit and Scrooge enter. Mrs. Cratchit feels a sudden draft.)* Oh, the wind. *(She gets up to shut the door.)*

SECOND SPIRIT

Hurry. *(He nudges Scrooge in before Mrs. Cratchit shuts the door.)*

SCROOGE

Hardly hospitable is what I'd say.

SECOND SPIRIT

Oh, they'd say a great deal more, Scrooge, if they could see you.

SCROOGE

Oh, they should, should they?

SECOND SPIRIT

Oh yes, I'd think they might.

SCROOGE

Well, I might have a word for them . . .

SECOND SPIRIT

You're here to listen.

SCROOGE

Oh. Oh yes, all right. By the fire?

SECOND SPIRIT

But not a word.

BOB CRATCHIT

(*raising his glass*) My dear, to Mr. Scrooge. I give you Mr. Scrooge, the founder of the feast.

MRS. CRATCHIT

The founder of the feast indeed! I wish I had him here! I'd give him a piece of my mind to feast upon, and I hope he'd have a good appetite for it.

BOB CRATCHIT

My dear, Christmas Eve.

MRS. CRATCHIT

It should be Christmas Eve, I'm sure, when one drinks the health of such an odious, stingy, hard, unfeeling man as Mr. Scrooge. You know he is, Robert! Nobody knows it better than you do, poor dear.

BOB CRATCHIT

I only know one thing on Christmas: that one must be charitable.

MRS. CRATCHIT

I'll drink to his health for your sake and the day's, not for his. Long life to him! A Merry Christmas and a Happy New Year. He'll be very merry and very happy, I have no doubt.

BOB CRATCHIT

If he cannot be, we must be happy for him. A song is what is needed. Tim!

MRS. CRATCHIT

Shush! I've just gotten him down and he needs all the sleep he can get.

BOB CRATCHIT

If he's asleep on Christmas Eve, I'll be much mistaken. Tim! He must sing, dear, there is nothing else that might make him well.

TINY TIM

Yes, Father?

BOB CRATCHIT

Are you awake?

TINY TIM

Just a little.

BOB CRATCHIT

A song then! (*The children awaken and, led by Tiny Tim, sit up to sing "What Child Is This?" As they sing, Scrooge speaks.*)

SCROOGE

Spirit. (*He holds up his hand; all stop singing and look at him.*) I . . . I have seen enough. (*When the spirit signals to the children, they leave the stage, singing the carol quietly. Tiny Tim remains, covered completely by the dark blanket, disappearing against the black.*) Tiny Tim . . . will he live?

SECOND SPIRIT

He is very ill. Even song cannot keep him whole through a cold winter.

SCROOGE

But you haven't told me!

SECOND SPIRIT

(*imitating Scrooge*) If he be like to die, he had better do it and decrease the surplus population. (*Scrooge turns away.*) Erase, Scrooge, those words from your thoughts. You are not the judge. Do not judge, then. It may be that in the sight of heaven you are more worthless and less fit to live than millions like this poor man's child. Oh God! To hear an insect on a leaf pronouncing that there is too much life among his hungry brothers in the dust. Good-bye, Scrooge.

SCROOGE

But is there no happiness in Christmas Present?

SECOND SPIRIT

There is.

SCROOGE

Take me there.

SECOND SPIRIT

It is at the home of your nephew . . .

SCROOGE

No!

SECOND SPIRIT

(*disgusted with Scrooge*) Then there is none.

SCROOGE

But that isn't enough . . . You must teach me!

SECOND SPIRIT

Would you have a teacher, Scrooge? Look at your own words.

SCROOGE

But the first spirit gave me more . . . !

SECOND SPIRIT

He was Christmas Past. There was a lifetime he could choose from. I have only this day, one day, and you, Scrooge. I have nearly lived my fill of both. Christmas Present must be gone at midnight. That is near now. (*He speaks to two beggar children who pause shyly at the far side of the stage. The children are thin and wan; they are barefoot and wear filthy rags.*) Come. (*They go to him.*)

SCROOGE

Is this the last spirit who is to come to me?

SECOND SPIRIT

They are no spirits. They are real. Hunger, Ignorance. Not spirits, Scrooge, passing dreams. They are real. They walk your streets, look to you for comfort. And you deny them. Deny them not too

long, Scrooge. They will grow and multiply and they will not
remain children.

SCROOGE

Have they no refuge, no resource?

SECOND SPIRIT

(*again imitating Scrooge*) Are there no prisons? Are there no
workhouses? (*tenderly to the children*) Come. It's Christmas Eve.
(*He leads them offstage.*)

Scene v   The Spirit of Christmas
Yet to Come

*Scrooge is entirely alone for a long moment. He is frightened by the
darkness and feels it approaching him. Suddenly he stops, senses the
presence of the third spirit, turns toward him, and sees him. The spirit
is bent and cloaked. No physical features are distinguishable.*

SCROOGE

You are the third. (*The spirit says nothing.*) The Ghost of Christmas Yet to Come. (*The spirit says nothing.*) Speak to me. Tell me
what is to happen — to me, to all of us. (*The spirit says nothing.*)
Then show me what I must see. (*The spirit points. Light illumines
the shadowy recesses of Scrooge's house.*) I know it. I know it too
well, cold and cheerless. It is mine. (*The cook and the charwoman
are dimly visible in Scrooge's house.*) What is . . . ? There
are . . . thieves! There are thieves in my rooms! (*He starts for-
ward to accost them, but the spirit beckons for him to stop.*) I
cannot. You cannot tell me that I must watch them and do nothing.
I will not. It is mine still. (*He rushes into the house to claim his*

belongings and to protect them. The two women do not notice his presence.)

COOK

He ain't about, is he? (*The charwoman laughs.*) Poor ol' Scrooge 'as met 'is end. (*She laughs with the charwoman.*)

CHARWOMAN

An' time for it, too; ain't been alive in deed for half his life.

COOK

But the Sparsit's nowhere, is he . . . ?

SPARSIT

(*emerging from the blackness*) Lookin' for someone, ladies? (*The cook shrieks, but the charwoman treats the matter more practically, anticipating competition from Sparsit.*)

CHARWOMAN

There ain't enough but for the two of us!

SPARSIT

More 'an enough . . . if you know where to look.

COOK

Hardly decent is what I'd say, hardly decent, the poor old fella hardly cold and you're thievin' his wardrobe.

SPARSIT

You're here out of love, are ya?

CHARWOMAN

There's no time for that. (*Sparsit acknowledges Scrooge for the first time, gesturing toward him as if the living Scrooge were the corpse. Scrooge stands as if rooted to the spot, held there by the power of the spirit.*)

SPARSIT

He ain't about to bother us, is he?

CHARWOMAN

Ain't he a picture?

COOK

If he is, it ain't a happy one. (*They laugh.*)

SPARSIT

Ladies, shall we start? (*The three of them grin and advance on Scrooge.*) Cook?

COOK

   (*snatching the cuff links from the shirt Scrooge wears*) They're gold, ain't they?

SPARSIT

   The purest, Madam.

CHARWOMAN

   I always had a fancy for that nightcap of his. My old man could use it. (*She takes the nightcap from Scrooge's head. Sparsit playfully removes Scrooge's outer garment, the coat or cloak that he has worn in the previous scenes.*)

SPARSIT

   Bein' a man of more practical tastes, I'll go for the worsted and hope the smell ain't permanent. (*The three laugh.*) Cook, we go round again.

COOK

   Do you think that little bell he's always ringing at me is silver enough to sell? (*The three of them move toward the nightstand and Scrooge cries out.*)

SCROOGE

   No more! No more! (*As the spirit directs Scrooge's attention to the tableau of the three thieves standing poised over the silver bell, Scrooge bursts out of the house, clad only in his nightshirt.*) I cannot. I cannot. The room is . . . too like a cheerless place that is familiar. I won't see it. Let us go from here. Anywhere. (*The spirit directs his attention to the Cratchit house; the children are sitting together near Mrs. Cratchit, who is sewing a coat. Peter reads by the light of the coals.*)

PETER

   "And he took a child and set him in the midst of them."

MRS. CRATCHIT

   (*putting her hand to her face*) The light tires my eyes so. (*pause*) They're better now. It makes them tired to try to see by firelight, and I wouldn't show reddened eyes to your father when he comes home for the world. It must be near his time now.

PETER

   Past it, I think, but he walks slower than he used to, these last few days, Mother.

MRS. CRATCHIT

I have known him to walk with . . . I have known him to walk with Tiny Tim upon his shoulder very fast indeed. (*She catches herself, then hurries on.*) But he was very light to carry and his father loved him so that it was no trouble, no trouble. (*She hears Bob Cratchit approaching.*) Smiles, everyone, smiles.

BOB CRATCHIT

(*entering*) My dear, Peter . . . (*He greets the other children by their real names.*) How is it coming?

MRS. CRATCHIT

(*handing him the coat*) Nearly done.

BOB CRATCHIT

Yes, good, I'm sure that it will be done long before Sunday.

MRS. CRATCHIT

Sunday! You went today then, Robert?

BOB CRATCHIT

Yes. It's . . . it's all ready. Two o'clock. And a nice place. It would have done you good to see how green it is. But you'll see it often. I promised him that, that I would walk there on Sunday . . . often.

MRS. CRATCHIT

We mustn't hurt ourselves for it, Robert.

BOB CRATCHIT

No. No, he wouldn't have wanted that. Come now. You won't guess who I've seen. Scrooge's nephew Fred. And he asked after us and said he was heartily sorry and to give his respect to my good wife. How he ever knew that, I don't know.

MRS. CRATCHIT

Knew what, my dear?

BOB CRATCHIT

Why, that you were a good wife.

PETER

Everybody knows that.

BOB CRATCHIT

I hope that they do. "Heartily sorry," he said, "for your good wife, and if I can be of service to you in any way — " and he gave me his card — "that's where I live" — and Peter, I shouldn't be at all surprised if he got you a position.

MRS. CRATCHIT

Only hear that, Peter!

BOB CRATCHIT

And then you'll be keeping company with some young girl and setting up for yourself.

PETER

Oh, go on.

BOB CRATCHIT

Well, it will happen, one day, but remember, when that day does come — as it must — we must none of us forget poor Tiny Tim and this first parting in our family.

SCROOGE

He died! No, no! (*He steps back and the scene disappears; he moves away from the spirit.*)

Scene vi   Scrooge's Conversion

SCROOGE

Because he would not . . . no! You cannot tell me that he has died, for that Christmas has not come! I will not let it come! I will be there . . . It was me. Yes, yes, and I knew it and couldn't look. I won't be able to help. I won't. (*pause*) Spirit, hear me. I am not the man I was. I will not be that man that I have been for so many years. Why show me all of this if I am past all hope? Assure me that I yet may change these shadows you have shown me. Let the boy live! I will honor Christmas in my heart and try to keep it all the year. I will live in the Past, the Present, and the Future. The spirits of all three shall strive within me. I will not shut out the lessons that they teach. Oh, tell me that I am not too late! (*A single light focuses on the little girl, dressed in a blue cloak like that of the Virgin Mary. She looks up, and from above a dove is slowly lowered in silence to her; she takes it and encloses it within her cloak, covering it. As soon as she does this, a large choir is heard singing "Gloria!" and the bells begin to ring. Blackout. When the lights come up again, Scrooge is in bed. The third spirit and the figures in the church have disappeared. Scrooge awakens and looks around his room.)* The curtains! They are mine and they are real. They are not sold. They are here. I am here, the shadows to come may be dispelled. They will be. I know they will be. *(He dresses himself hurriedly.)* I don't know what to do. I'm as light as a feather, merry as a boy again. Merry Christmas! Merry Christmas! A Happy New Year to all the world! Hello there! Whoop! Hallo! What day of the month is it? How long did the spirits keep me? Never mind. I don't care. *(He opens the window and calls to a boy in the street below.)* What's today?

BOY

Eh?

SCROOGE

What's the day, my fine fellow?

BOY

Today? Why, Christmas Day!

SCROOGE

It's Christmas Day! I haven't missed it! The spirits have done it all in one night. They can do anything they like. Of course they can. Of course they can save Tim. Hallo, my fine fellow!

BOY

Hallo!

SCROOGE

Do you know the poulterers in the next street at the corner?

BOY

I should hope I do.

SCROOGE

An intelligent boy. A remarkable boy. Do you know whether they've sold the prize turkey that was hanging up there? Not the little prize; the big one.

BOY

What, the one as big as me?

SCROOGE

What a delightful boy! Yes, my bucko!

BOY

It's hanging there now.

SCROOGE

It is? Go and buy it.

BOY

G'wan!

SCROOGE

I'm in earnest! Go and buy it and tell 'em to bring it here that I may give them the direction where to take it. Come back with the butcher and I'll give you a shilling. Come back in less than two minutes and I'll give you half a crown!

BOY

Right, guv! (*He exits.*)

SCROOGE

I'll send it to Bob Cratchit's. He shan't know who sends it. It's twice the size of Tiny Tim and such a Christmas dinner it will make. (*Carolers suddenly appear singing "Hark! The Herald Angels Sing." Scrooge leans out the window and joins them in the song.*) I must dress, I must. It's Christmas Day! I must be all in my best for such a day. Where is my China silk shirt? (*The boy and the butcher run in with the turkey.*) What? Back already? And such a turkey. Why, you can't carry that all the way to Cratchit's. Here, boy, here is your half a crown and here an address in Camden town. See that it gets there. Here, money for the cab, for the turkey, and for you, good man! (*The boy and the butcher, delighted, catch the money and run out. Scrooge sees the gentleman visitor walking by the window.*) Halloo, sir!

GENTLEMAN VISITOR

(*looking up sadly, less than festive*) Hello, sir.

SCROOGE

My dear sir, how do you do? I hope you succeeded yesterday. It was very kind of you to stop by to see me.

GENTLEMAN VISITOR

(*in disbelief*) Mr. Scrooge?

SCROOGE

Yes, that is my name and I fear it may not be pleasant to you. Allow me to ask your pardon, and will you have the goodness to add this (*throwing him a purse*) to your good work!

GENTLEMAN VISITOR

Lord bless me! My dear Mr. Scrooge, are you serious?

SCROOGE

If you please, not a penny less. A great many back payments are included in it, I assure you. Will you do me that favor?

GENTLEMAN VISITOR

My dear sir, I don't know what I can say to such generosity . . .

SCROOGE

Say nothing! Accept it. Come and see me. Will you come and see me?

GENTLEMAN VISITOR

I will.

SCROOGE

Thank 'ee. I am much obliged to you. I thank you fifty times. God bless you and Merry Christmas!

GENTLEMAN VISITOR

Merry Christmas to you, sir!

SCROOGE

(*running downstairs, out of his house, and onto the street*) Now which is the way to that nephew's house. Girl! Girl!

GIRL

(*appearing immediately*) Yes, sir?

SCROOGE

Can you find me a taxi, miss?

GIRL

I can, sir. (*She rings her doll and a coachman appears.*)

SCROOGE

(*handing the coachman a card*) Can you show me the way to this home?

COACHMAN

I can, sir.

SCROOGE

> Good man. Come up, girl. (*They mount to the top of the taxi. This action may be stylistically suggested.*) Would you be an old man's guide to a Christmas dinner?

GIRL

> I would, sir, and God bless you!

SCROOGE

> Yes, God bless us every one! (*raising his voice almost in song*) Driver, to Christmas! (*They exit, all three singing "Joy to the World." Blackout. The lights come up for the finale, a music and dance reprise of "Fezziwig's Party,"* this time at Fred's house. The Cratchits are there with Tiny Tim. All stop moving and talking when they see Scrooge standing in the center, embarrassed and humble.*) Well, I'm very glad to be here at my nephew's house! (*He starts to cry.*) Merry Christmas! Merry Christmas!

ALL

> (*softly*) Merry Christmas. (*They sing "Deck the Halls," greeting one another and exchanging gifts. Scrooge puts Tiny Tim on his shoulders.*)

TINY TIM

> (*shouting as the carol ends*) God bless us every one!

SCROOGE

> (*to the audience*) Oh, yes! God bless us every one!

*Music on pages 52–55.

A Christmas Carol. ''No more work tonight!''
(Photograph by Don Yunker.)

Fezziwig's Party

NOTE: Music for *A Christmas Carol* composed by Scott Crosbie.

Continued on next page

The Legend of Sleepy Hollow

Adapted by Frederick Gaines

ICHABOD

> *. . . despite my attempts at education,*
> *the residents of this sleepy town persist in the belief in*
> *the supernatural. The neighborhood abounds with*
> *tales, twilight superstitions, haunted spots. Stars shoot*
> *and meteors glare oftener across their valley than in*
> *any other part of the country, and the nightmare, with*
> *her whole ninefold, makes it the favorite scene of her*
> *gambols. There is even a legend about a Headless*
> *Horseman, but as with all the rest: it is nonsense.*

This adaptation of Washington Irving's *The Legend of Sleepy Hollow* was first produced by the Children's Theatre Company of the Minneapolis Society of Fine Arts in October 1969. The script was edited by Linda Walsh Jenkins with the assistance of Carol K. Metz.

Cast of Characters

Ichabod Crane	Katrina Van Tassel
Widow Winetraub	Ichabod's students
Hilda Winetraub	The Sleepy Hollow Boys
Townspeople	Pastor
Cornwall	Van Ripper
Brom Bones (Brom Van Brunt)	Actor-image of Ichabod

Sequence of Scenes

Scene i	Nonsense, Master Crane?
Scene ii	Psalmody and Brom's Tale
Scene iii	There Are No Witches!
Scene iv	The Sleepy Hollow Boys
Scene v	Strudel and Gremlins
Scene vi	Sunday Courting
Scene vii	Preparing for the Party
Scene viii	The Van Tassels' Party
Scene ix	The Ride of the Headless Horseman
Scene x	Finale

Notes on the Play

In the opening scene Ichabod Crane, schoolteacher and singing master, lectures against illogical superstition, but it immediately becomes apparent that superstition rules the life of Sleepy Hollow. Ichabod is never safe from the whispers of fear which pursue him whether he is courting Katrina, free-loading on his neighbors' hospitality, or lecturing to his music students. Though the fears seem fanciful and the fun intentional, their effect on Ichabod is the effect always felt by the person who is the butt of a joke, the one who lets the audience laugh. Throughout the play Ichabod rarely leaves the stage, and while there he talks incessantly; yet much of Irving's elaborate prose has been replaced with wordless actions. Gaines's cinematic storytelling emphasizes the dreamlike flow and pace of Ichabod's nightmare.

The central feature in the design of the set is a sweeping boardwalk that curves to the floor at downstage center and sweeps upward at stage left. The platform is raked at the center so that the action is thrust toward the audience. The boards are gray and weathered like those of an old bridge. A large tree rises along the proscenium on the right, and its branches extend across the top of the proscenium. There is another tree at upstage right behind the platform. The stage palette is of warm fall colors. A leaf bag (similar to that used to create the effect of falling snow) occasionally sets autumn leaves swirling onto the platform. No stage furniture is used; a board in the left slope of the platform swings up to form a bench in a few scenes. Very few props are needed because the actors "furnish" the stage with pantomime (holding hymnals, spreading picnic cloths, and so forth). The costumes are based on seventeenth-century Dutch styles with exaggerated silhouettes which add to the humorous bearing of the pixillated colonial characters.

Scene i   Nonsense, Master Crane?

As the play opens, Ichabod is hurrying away from a sound he believes is following him. He stops to address the audience.

ICHABOD

As schoolmaster of this village . . . (*A noise makes him jump; he listens for a moment and then continues.*) As schoolmaster, I deal in simple fact, and the simple fact is that there's no such things as ghosts . . . (*His voice breaks on the word "ghosts" and goes upward in pitch; he brings it under control.*) That is, ghosts. (*He clears his throat and continues.*) Ghosts are superstitious explanations for unexplainable phenomena, but I, as a dealer in simple fact, say to you that behind those phenomena . . . (*He hears a melancholy moaning sound produced by someone blowing across the neck of an empty jug. He stops and listens; the moaning ceases.*) Yes. Behind the phenomena is a common, everyday occurrence . . . (*The moaning begins again, accompanied by the sound of creaking boards.*) There are some who would hear in that melancholy sound the footsteps of a ghost, but I, of course, hear nothing . . . like . . . it. (*He turns fearfully to face the approaching sound. A young man with a jug appears and strolls past Ichabod, who is greatly relieved.*) As I said before: an everyday occurrence. Yet despite my attempts at education, the residents of this sleepy town persist in the belief in the supernatural. The neighborhood abounds with tales, twilight superstitions,

60

haunted spots. Stars shoot and meteors glare oftener across their valley than in any other part of the country, and the nightmare, with her whole ninefold, makes it the favorite scene of her gambols. There is even a legend about a Headless Horseman, but as with all the rest: it is nonsense. (*Widow Winetraub enters with a large picnic hamper on one arm and plump, blushing Hilda on the other. She immediately determines where they are to picnic and begins to spread the cloth.*)

WIDOW

Nonsense, Master Crane? Nonsense? What I could tell you! But a man of your importance has other things to think of, I'm sure. Nonsense? If my poor departed husband were here, "Nonsense," he'd tell you, I'm sure! Hmph!

ICHABOD

Oh, but Widow Winetraub, could a legend have hurt him? Oh, no, it seems unlikely.

WIDOW

Yes, yes, I told them that — cider, Master Crane? — but who would listen to me, a simple woman. You've met my daughter, Master Crane? (*Ichabod nods and doffs his hat in gentlemanly fashion. Hilda giggles and blushes.*) Died of fright, they say — cinnamon, Master Crane? — Died of the sight of the Headless Horseman.

ICHABOD

Died of the . . . ?

WIDOW

(*nodding emphatically*) Well, I laughed. Laughed right out loud. But there he lay, Master Crane, white as flour, Master Crane . . . (*Ichabod mouths the question, "White as flour?" and she nods once, sharply.*) White as flour, Master. Hilda made the cider, Master Crane.

ICHABOD

(*eating with desperate energy*) Oh, did she? Very good, very good indeed . . .

WIDOW

So what was I to say, Master Crane, with all of them against me, poor widow that I am and my only daughter still unmarried? What was I to say, Master Crane? Well, I don't know. Master Crane says there's no such thing as ghosts and that to you, I should of said, but could I think of that? Pass the man some cakes, Hilda, don't be such a bump.

ICHABOD

Well, Widow Winetraub . . .

WIDOW

That's all very well to say, Master Crane, but I've not your learning, your way with words and arguments. My daughter admires you a great deal, Master Crane, don't you, daughter?

HILDA

(*blushing*) Ma!

WIDOW

I know if I had the power of tongue I've heard you so often display, I should have disputed them in a minute, but I, speechless and defenseless, so to speak. You do understand what I mean, Master Crane?

ICHABOD

(*his mouth full of cake*) I believe I do, Widow Winetraub.

WIDOW

I should have said what you've said to me, but with a poor, cold, stone-dead husband lying there who was hale and hearty an hour before . . .

ICHABOD

Hale and hearty . . .

WIDOW

Hale, Master Crane . . . (*Ichabod, unable to speak the portentous word, mouths it.*) And hearty. Well! It would have sounded stupid as all get out, Master Crane. Have a pipe, Master Crane. (*She hands him a clay pipe.*)

ICHABOD

Oh, I don't know . . .

WIDOW

Don't myself, but my poor husband, poor frightened-to-death

man, always felt fondly toward the habit. I like to put a man at ease, Master Crane; smoke.

ICHABOD

Thank you very much, Widow, but you see, my voice, the singing lessons, you understand. (*He sings a note or two to demonstrate for her.*)

WIDOW

Doesn't seem likely it'll do great harm, Master Crane.

ICHABOD

Well, a pipe's a fond pleasure after a fine meal . . . (*The long-stemmed Dutch pipe is forced upon him.*)

WIDOW

Good for digestion, Master Crane, rheumatiz, melancholy, and sour stomach. My husband's own blend.

ICHABOD

The pipe's your . . . husband's?

WIDOW

(*forcing the pipe into Ichabod's mouth*) Last thing he did before he died; smoked it.

ICHABOD

Thank you all the same, but it's a long ride. Hardly enough time now. Widow Winetraub . . . (*He rises to leave.*)

WIDOW

You forgot my daughter. Smile at the man, Daughter. (*She and Hilda rise and curtsy. Two and three at a time, the townspeople begin to enter on the ramp. They walk as if out for a stroll in the fall, pointing at leaves and birds. They speak in a low murmur, ignoring Ichabod, the widow, and Hilda.*)

ICHABOD

Hilda. I can only say, I wish my appointed rounds were less strict. Your cider, your pipe, your daughter all tempt me, but psalmody calls me.

WIDOW

I think you're some kind of a fool, Master Crane. (*All the townspeople are onstage and only a few steps away from chorus position by the time Ichabod says "their eyes following my baton.")*

ICHABOD

I thank you for the hospitality, the food, but could I disappoint them? They await my instruction, their voices poised, their eyes following my baton . . . And music is born. (*As Ichabod conducts from center stage, using the pipe as a baton, the chorus begins to sing.*)

Scene ii   Psalmody and Brom's Tale

All the townspeople are in a semicircle on the ramp facing Ichabod; they appear to be sitting, holding songbooks. As they sing, they move up and down like organ keys in a rigidly choreographed sequence. As Ichabod says "born," he gives a strong beat, the organ plays, and the chorus begins to sing. During the song Ichabod walks among the chorus members, listening, adjusting mouths, criticizing, and lecturing.

CHORUS

> *The Lord sings out!*
> *The Lord sings out!*
> *The Lord sings out, and His blessings fall upon us!*
> *The Lord sings out!*
> *The Lord sings out!*
> *The Lord sings out, and His bounty falls upon us!*
> *Sing out His praise!*
> *Sing out His praise!*
> *Sing out His praise, Jerusalem!*

The Lord sings out!
The Lord sings out . . .
(*Ichabod cuts off the singing by tapping on the rostrum with his pipe.*)

ICHABOD

Please, please. Excellent voice, full of spirit, but we-must-learn-to-sing-together. Each word must be clipped and e-nun-ci-a-ted. Understood? Good. Now, to the art of singing psalmody. Many will say that song (*he gives them a note; they immediately hum it, and then he cuts them off*) is song. But, of course, there is art to the psalmody of psalm singing. Now, voice is, of course, pleasant to listen to, but more important than voice is pitch. As thus. (*He listens, concentrating, and sings "hmmm," missing the note completely but entirely satisfied with his effort.*) Yes. Now, you, please. (*He points to a member of the chorus who sings the note as it should be. Ichabod gives a grudging approval. He sounds the note again, off pitch.*) "Hmmm!" Now, all. (*The chorus sings a full, rich chord. He cuts them off again abruptly.*) Where — we must ask ourselves — where does music begin? And the answer is, of course, within the nose. The nose. In the nose is a vibrating chamber which we in music call the nasal drum. (*He walks into the chorus and questions a boy.*) What do we call it?

BOY

Drum.

ICHABOD

(*to a girl*) What?

GIRL

Drum. Nasal drum.

ICHABOD

(*approaching Katrina*) Ah, Katrina . . . Plum pudding? (*She smiles. Ichabod returns to the front of the group.*) When the nasal drum is set into vibration, "hmmmymmmmmmmy" . . . (*The members of the chorus try to make this sound, but he cuts them off.*) The sound begins here and travels through here, into the cheeks, perimeterates the lips, and out the mouth. (*He points to a boy.*) The what?

ICHABOD

BOY

Mouth.

ICHABOD

The mouth. Thus. (*He demonstrates what he has just described, showing the progress of a whine with his fingers. The members of the chorus follow his example.*) Now, in the psalm . . . (*He cuts them off so he can be heard.*) Now, in the psalm "The Lord Sings Out" . . . (*Cornwall hurries in, trying to be unobtrusive; he moves through the ranks of the chorus, disturbing the symmetry as he passes through.*) You're late.

CORNWALL

Yes, sir, sorry, sir. (*Ichabod waits conspicuously for Cornwall to get to his place before continuing.*)

ICHABOD

Now. In the psalm "The Lord Sings Out," the nasal drum, or cavity, as we in the anatomical anthropology call it, plays an important role . . .

CORNWALL

(*whispering to his neighbor*) Brom Bones raced against the Headless Horseman. (*The members of the chorus begin whispering among themselves as the word is passed. Ichabod continues to talk, facing away from them. Each time he turns to them, they act as if nothing had happened. A look of both curiosity and annoyance passes over Ichabod's face, but he tries to maintain his dignity.*)

ICHABOD

Beginning with the sound "rrrd" in "Lorrrd" . . . (*He catches them whispering; they stop. He tries to ignore it.*) And into the "ying" sound of "singggg" . . . (*He catches them again. He turns away and they start talking again.*) Gentlemen, gentlemen! (*He raps with his pipe. They stop whispering for a moment, but as soon as Ichabod resumes the lecture, the news continues to spread quickly through the entire chorus. Ichabod's lecture becomes more and more disjointed.*) The hard consonant "rrrud," or, as we in phonics call it, the "rud" sound: We allow the nasal tone to build and increase . . . (*He tries to overhear what is being gossiped and loses the thread of his lecture.*) Multiplying in propensity, resonating in pitch and fiber, the fourth phonic, or *rebusto*, as we in the stage art refer to it . . . If that is so, then we must ask our-selves: wherefore the Dielanzzo? (*pointing to Cornwall*) Young man! (*All stop whispering and lean toward Cornwall.*)

CORNWALL

Yes, sir?

ICHABOD

What trifle of gossip could possibly be so edifying and full of import . . . ?

CORNWALL

(*to the whole chorus*) Brom Bones raced against the Headless Horseman! (*As the members of the chorus gasp, Brom Bones enters and strolls to the center.*)

ICHABOD

Brom Bones!

BROM

It was nothing.

FIRST CHORUS

Where was it?

BROM

Sleepy Hollow graveyard.

SECOND CHORUS

The covered bridge?

BROM

Yes.

THIRD CHORUS

Did you see him?

BROM

I saw him.

FOURTH CHORUS

Did he have . . . (*They are afraid to finish.*)

BROM

> (*shaking his head*) No head. (*The members of the chorus suddenly begin to tell the story of the race as a group event, something they have all shared in, passing the story from one to another. "Brom's Tale"* is performed as a choral story in which the voices also create onomatopoetic sound effects. Dim lights and organ music add to the mood of suspense and midnight terror.*)

FIFTH CHORUS

> Dark as sin and not a sound. Midnight. Bats flapping. (*The chorus as a group whispers "bats flapping . . . bats flapping . . ."*) Owls hooting. (*The members of the chorus hoot like owls.*)

SIXTH CHORUS

> And along he came, poor Brom Bones, into the graveyard. You could hear the graves a-moaning. (*The chorus moans.*) But not a sound from Brom.

BROM

> (*with false modesty*) I was kind of sleepy, dozing a little.

FIRST CHORUS

> And then you heard . . . hoofbeats! (*One member of the chorus begins to make the sound of slow, menacing hoofbeats on his knees. Everybody focuses on Brom. They syncopate the dialogue with the steadily increasing pace of the hoofbeats.*)

SECOND CHORUS

> Whadja do?

BROM

> I kind of turned to see what's what.

THIRD CHORUS

> There . . . in the shadows . . .

FOURTH CHORUS

> . . . was a man on a horse . . . (*The entire chorus echoes "horse . . . horse . . ."*)

THIRD CHORUS

> Standin' eighteen hands . . .

*Music on pages 100–103.

ICHABOD

(*echoing*) Eighteen hands . . .

CHORUS

The Horseman! (*The pace of the hoofbeats increases, building to a gallop.*)

FOURTH CHORUS

Breathin' fire . . .

FIFTH CHORUS

Black as coal . . .

SIXTH CHORUS

His eyes red-yellow! He had hooves of steel!

ICHABOD

(*echoing*) Of steel . . .

FIRST CHORUS

Asittin' him calm as death . . .

SECOND CHORUS

. . . is a hooded shape! (*The hoofbeats stop.*)

CHORUS

No-o-o-o head! Slowly . . . slowly . . . slowly . . .

SECOND CHORUS

He raised hisself, standin' in his stirrups ten feet tall, and he pointed his hand off toward the bridge.

BROM

To the bridge.

CHORUS

The bridge!

SEVERAL CHORUSES

Hurry! Hurry! Hurry! (*The hoofbeats begin again, breaking into a fast gallop.*)

FIRST CHORUS

The Horseman and Brom side by side . . .

SECOND CHORUS

Brom and the Devil ridin' for a prize . . .

ICHABOD

Ridin' through the woods of Sleepy Hollow!

WOMEN

In the middle of the ride . . .

MEN

Old Brom bellows . . .

BROM

(*shouting*) A bowl of punch to the winner!

CHORUS

Ahhhhh . . . (*The drumming of the hoofbeats is even faster now, a fully extended gallop. The chorus pants the lines until the blackout.*)

FIRST CHORUS

Three furlongs . . .

SECOND CHORUS

Two to go!

THIRD CHORUS

Two furlongs . . .

FOURTH CHORUS

One to go!

ICHABOD

Covered bridge is just ahead . . .

FIFTH CHORUS

Brom's horse is pulling ahead . . .

SIXTH CHORUS

Twenty yards . . .

FIRST CHORUS

Ten yards . . .

ALL

Five to go!

ICHABOD

Lunging for his life . . . (*Ichabod, totally caught up in the account of the ride, clings to Brom. The hoofbeats stop.*)

BROM

(*calmly, deflating the climactic moment*) Brom crosses the line. (*The chorus snickers at Ichabod.*) And he was gone. Not a trace. Smell of brimstone and fire, nothing more.

FIFTH CHORUS
No punch?

BROM
(*laughing*) No punch. But I beat him square. He won't ride this way for a while. (*The chorus cheers.*)

ICHABOD
I don't believe a word. (*The chorus laughs.*) I don't. All that nonsense of Headless Horsemen and riding phantoms is nonsense. It's all in the book I have. Master Cotton Mather's book. You've only to sing a psalm, Master Mather says, and the very devil will run from you. Sing a psalm loud and clear, and the strongest of ghosts will turn tail. (*People begin to walk slowly offstage, their hands folded in prayer. The organ plays "The Lord Sings Out" and they mouth the words, ignoring Ichabod. He tries to get their attention, following them out.*) As schoolmaster, I feel it's my duty to instruct you in such matters and to warn you against . . . (*He exits. Katrina and Brom remain onstage. Katrina starts to follow the others, but Brom takes her arm, turning her toward him.*)

KATRINA
You're very familiar, Master Van Brunt.

BROM
As familiar as the smile from your singing master?

KATRINA
That is none of your concern.

BROM
I make it my concern.

KATRINA
Do you, Master Van Brunt!

BROM
You've called me Brom before . . .

KATRINA
In the past.

BROM
There's been nothing to change that.

KATRINA

My mind has changed.

BROM

And it's been changed by that gangle Crane!

KATRINA

Master Crane is not a . . . whatever you call him. He is a gentleman, and that is considerably more than some storytellers that I know.

BROM

There's no harm in a story.

KATRINA

There is harm in a lie. You sat in our parlor till midnight or past, Master Van Brunt, and I doubt you met your Horseman there.

BROM

(*hedging*) It might have been a bit after midnight . . .

KATRINA

The stories you tell are that the ghost never rides past midnight.

BROM

Past dawn, past dawn is what I've always said!

KATRINA

You can think up the answers before I can think of the questions. Good day, Master Storyteller. (*She turns and leaves abruptly.*)

BROM

I meant no harm with it. You know me better than to think that . . . (*He follows her offstage just as Ichabod enters with a book containing the writings of Cotton Mather.*)

Scene iii   There Are No Witches!

ICHABOD

(*his nose buried in the book*) Diverse incidents lead us to believe in
the . . . (*looking up*) Miss Katrina? Katrina? (*He sees that he is
alone.*) Gone. And with Brom, too. I should have read him such
an argument . . . Cotton Mather's book . . . Well. Chil-
ly . . . (*Ichabod puts the book under his arm, claps his hat
on his head, and starts off toward his rooms at Van Ripper's.
Whistling, he pretends not to notice the darkness around him. As
he walks along the boardwalk, he steps on a loose board that emits
an organ tone. He stops, uncertain where the sound has come
from. He slowly retraces his steps and again hits the loose board;
he jumps as the organ note sounds again. He gingerly depresses
the board with his foot and the note sounds. Reassured, almost
playfully, he depresses it several times with his foot, then carefully
straddles the loose board, leans over it, and plays it with his
finger. Smiling, unafraid again, he starts to walk on past the loose
board, but halfway down the boardwalk a thought begins to pester
him; he returns to the approximate area, no longer certain which
is the loose board. He finally steps on the board, it sounds, and he
quickly steps to the far side of it. The organ sounds again, the next
"stop" up the keyboard. Ichabod tries to get off the protesting
boards, but each step he makes, on either side of the original
board, causes another organ note to sound. He spraddles his legs
farther and farther apart, but the whole boardwalk has become
possessed. He tries to escape it, running up to the high point of the
boardwalk-keyboard. He stands, perched on his tiptoes on the last
board, almost offstage, the organ shrilling. He loses his balance*

and stumbles down the boardwalk-keyboard; a cascade of organ notes parallels his descent until he falls at the very spot where the loose board is and the organ roars a thunderous cacophony. Quickly he pulls out his book by Mather and hurriedly thumbs through its index.) "Screams," "sirens," "sobs," "sounds" . . . ah! "sounds in the night"! "See the case of the Salem witches." Salem . . . Salem . . . (*The first student slowly enters behind Ichabod and stands beside him as he says "sixteen ninety-one."*) Here we are. In Salem, Massachusetts, in sixteen ninety-one . . .

FIRST STUDENT

The witches were hung. (*Ichabod looks at him; the student tries to clarify the statement.*) In sixteen ninety-one, sir, the Salem witch trials. Governor Danforth . . . (*Other boys slowly come in.*)

ICHABOD

Not another word. There are no witches. Period. End of discussion. (*At this point the boys are in place on the slope of the ramp, seated, as if in school. The first student joins them.*) Now where were we?

SECOND STUDENT

History lesson, sir.

ICHABOD

Ah, yes, history. Fourteen ninety-two . . .

STUDENTS

Columbus sailed the blue!

ICHABOD

Fourteen ninety-three. He . . .

STUDENTS

Sailed across the sea!

ICHABOD

(*pointing to one student after another as he gives the dates*) Seventeen hundred and seventy-five . . .

THIRD STUDENT

At Bunker Hill, we come alive!

ICHABOD

Seventeen hundred and seventy-six . . .

FOURTH STUDENT
> Repel Old George . . .

STUDENTS
> . . . with stones and sticks! (*Ichabod's confidence is returning;
> he singles out individual students, using his walking stick like a
> sword, dancing through the fencing positions as he chooses stu-
> dents to answer.*)

ICHABOD
> Seventeen hundred and seventy-seven . . .

FIFTH STUDENT
> Articles of Confederation!

ICHABOD
> Seventeen hundred and seventy-eight . . .

STUDENTS
> America and France form an alliance! Force the British to com-
> pliance!

ICHABOD
> How do you spell compliance? (*no answer*) You don't know be-
> cause I haven't taught you yet. (*He turns to Cornwall.*) Seventeen
> hundred and seventy-nine . . .

CORNWALL
> Uh . . . (*Slight pause. Ichabod parries with his walking stick
> touching Cornwall's chest.*)

ICHABOD
> Seventeen hundred and seventy-nine? (*Cornwall still hesitates.
> Ichabod dances backward and forward, playfully.*) Seventy-nine?
> (*After a slight pause he addresses the first student.*) Do you like
> apples?

FIRST STUDENT
> Yes, sir.

ICHABOD
> So do I. (*to Cornwall*) Seventeen hundred and seventy-nine! (*He
> starts to lunge with his stick.*)

CORNWALL
> (*desperately*) Major André in the pine! (*The class gasps.*)

ICHABOD

Who, Master Scholar, who?

CORNWALL

Major André, sir, he's in the book.

ICHABOD

And what did he do?

CORNWALL

Died, sir.

ICHABOD

What, sir?

CORNWALL

Died, sir.

ICHABOD

Why, sir?

CORNWALL

Spy, sir, please, sir, with Benedict Arnold, and they caught him.

ICHABOD

Twenty lashes!

CORNWALL

By the tree, sir, in Sleepy Hollow, sir, and they hung him high . . . (*Ichabod stops. Silence.*) By the neck, sir. Till he's dead. And his ghost . . .

STUDENTS

Ohhhh, ooohhhh . . .

ICHABOD

Twenty lashes! (*He hurries the boy away and warns the class to be quiet. He pantomimes opening a door, pushing the boy out.*) And not a word from any of you. Not a word. (*He follows Cornwall to one side of the stage. Several boys go to the "door" and crouch to listen to the punishment being meted out. Ichabod brandishes his walking stick.*) Twenty lashes . . .

STUDENTS

(*counting, breathless*) Four, five, six . . .

ICHABOD

Twenty lashes . . .

STUDENTS
Seven, eight, nine . . .

ICHABOD
Twenty lashes . . .

FIRST STUDENT
Ichabod Crane can't hurt a flea!

STUDENTS
Ten, eleven, twelve . . .

SECOND STUDENT
Ichabod Crane can't hurt me!

ICHABOD
Twenty lashes . . .

THIRD STUDENT
Ichabod Crane's a skinny chicken, sits in the kitchen, talking to women! Ichabod's skinny nose itches, if he hears a sound like witches!

STUDENTS
Thirteen, fourteen, fifteen . . .

ICHABOD
Twenty lashes . . . (*Several students run around, shrieking.*)

STUDENTS
Four to go, three to go . . .

ICHABOD
Twenty lashes . . .

STUDENTS
One to go, done! (*The students rush back to their seats. Ichabod and Cornwall return, and Cornwall goes to his seat.*)

ICHABOD
So? Frightened, am I? Itchy nose, have I? Well, scholars, we shall see what we shall see. I care not a pinch for your ghosts and goblins! (*He makes a dashing affirmative gesture. He turns away from them to brag.*) Your common witch knows better than to traffic with the likes of Ichabod Crane! (*All the boys make goblin faces behind his back. Ichabod stops short, looks at them, then away. They stop making faces; he looks back at them.*) If your

garden variety witch so much as crosses my path, out comes my Master Mather and off flies the witch. And not on a broomstick, either. God made the birds to fly and no one else . . . (*A student has turned into a goblin. The other students appear to be unaware of the transformation. Ichabod is beginning to be concerned. He is afraid to look at them.*) That is not to say witches do not exist. Only the ignorant would swear to such a positive declaration . . . (*He turns quickly to see if another goblin has appeared. Now there are three goblins. He turns away again.*) The wise say . . . I doubt it . . . I doubt it. I seem to be a little . . . weary . . . Class dismissed. (*The boys run off, celebrating. Ichabod stands transfixed. Cornwall remains behind.*)

CORNWALL

Sir?

ICHABOD

(*terrified*) Oh, my goodness! Oh, my (*more calmly, seeing that it is a student*) goodness!

CORNWALL

Master Crane?

ICHABOD

Yes, my boy, speak right up. Nothing to be frightened of. Master Crane is here to protect you.

CORNWALL

You said, sir, to tell you when next my mother baked.

ICHABOD

And does she today?

CORNWALL

Pies, sir, and bread.

ICHABOD

(*his mouth watering*) Pies? What kind?

CORNWALL

Mince, sir, raisin, and pumpkin.

ICHABOD

And apple?

CORNWALL
> Yes, sir. (*Ichabod relaxes and smiles, knowing the boy wants to please him.*)

ICHABOD
> Berry?

CORNWALL
> Yes, sir.

ICHABOD
> Cherry? Quince?

CORNWALL
> I think so, sir.

ICHABOD
> Plum? Gooseberry? Mulberry? Rhubarb? Banana?

CORNWALL
> I . . .

ICHABOD
> Banana?

CORNWALL
> I . . . hope so, sir.

ICHABOD
> You're a bright lad.

CORNWALL
> Yes, sir.

ICHABOD
> A boy to be proud of . . .

CORNWALL
> Yes, sir.

ICHABOD
> Shall we walk?

CORNWALL
> Yes, sir.

ICHABOD
> See that tree over there? Orioles. Four eggs last spring.

CORNWALL
> Yes, sir.

ICHABOD

And what do you make of all of this nonsense?

CORNWALL

School, sir?

ICHABOD

No, no. Ghosts and goblins and all like that.

CORNWALL

I don't believe an inch of 'em, sir.

ICHABOD

You don't?

CORNWALL

No, sir. Witches don't exist, sir. Except for Halloween, for an hour or two. (*They walk up the boardwalk.*)

ICHABOD

Good boy. That one there, sir, what is it?

CORNWALL

Blue jay, I think, sir. (*They reach the top of the boardwalk hill, and there is Katrina with two of her friends. The girls laugh and talk together. Ichabod looks at Katrina, then shoos the boy toward home.*)

ICHABOD

Quite right, a jay.

CORNWALL

What shall I tell her about the pies, sir?

ICHABOD

(*still looking at Katrina*) Tell her I won't . . . be long. (*Cornwall exits. Ichabod takes Katrina's arm, and they walk down the boardwalk. Ichabod, infatuated, entertains the girls gallantly.*)

Scene iv   The Sleepy Hollow Boys

The Sleepy Hollow Boys saunter in, carrying jugs and singing to evoke the sound of a tune played on empty jugs. They take their places around the ramp, carelessly slouching, leaning against the tree and each other. Brom has just outlined a plan.

BROM

And I'll take Master Crane, myself. (*Widow Winetraub is heard laughing offstage.*) They're coming. (*The Sleepy Hollow Boys slip behind the ramp and hide under it. Some are seen by the audience but not by the widow and Hilda.*)

WIDOW

And would you listen to your mother?

HILDA

But, Ma . . .

WIDOW

"No, I know best," you say, "I'll send a little boy with a penny." And where's the little boy and the penny? Both gone and no Master Crane in sight. You'll be the death of me. I swear you will. I feel weaker already. I'd better sit.

HILDA

But, Ma . . .

WIDOW

"But, Ma." You sound like a goose been stepped on. Like a lady, Hilda, softly, like your mama. Spread your shawl, girl. You want your dying mother sittin' on a board? (*Hilda spreads out her shawl, and the widow sits down on the edge of the boardwalk. The Sleepy Hollow Boys make bird sounds.*)

HILDA

No, Ma.

WIDOW

You're a shameful girl, Hilda, shameful. Never listen to a word your poor old widowed mother says. Fatten him up, I say, spread out the sweets, I say, and the schoolteacher will come like bees to honey. And what do you do? Send a schoolboy to speak for you with a made-up story of his mother baking pies. Speak for yourself, that's what I say. There's not a bit of immodesty in a girl extending an invitation to supper, not a bit. (*While she rattles on, Brom says "Hssst!" and a member of the gang sneaks up behind Hilda, drags her off the boardwalk, and hides her away. Her mother keeps on talking.*) Master Crane would have thought it no more than friendliness. You know how fond of his eating is Master Crane. The whole Hollow knows how fond of his eating Master Crane is. He eats a great deal, you could say he eats too much, far too much; you could say that he's a pig at a trough and not be far off, but we don't like to find fault, Hildy. Catch as catch can, I always say. If you took after your mother, it might be a different matter, but you're plain as cottage cheese, girl, a turnip, and we can't be too particular, can we? Hildy? (*One of the Sleepy Hollow Boys imitates the croak of a frog from under the bridge.*) Hildy? Now, where'd that girl get to? (*She stomps away to shout offstage.*) Hilda! I'll be switched. If that doesn't beat all . . . (*The frog croaks again. The widow stops, then moves toward the sound. Silence. From the other side of the bridge comes Hilda's muffled voice. The widow hurries toward the sound, but one of the boys utters a quack to mask Hilda's voice.*) Ducks. Hildy? (*Hilda's muffled voice is heard again. The widow decides Hilda has gone under the bridge. She lifts her skirts and gingerly steps down into the water.*) I swan, that girl will be the death of me (*a boy sneaks up behind her and gives her a solid push, and she is quickly pulled out of sight by the other members of the gang*) yet!! (*The moment the widow disappears, Katrina and Ichabod enter. Katrina is hurrying away with Ichabod in pursuit, imploring her.*)

ICHABOD

It was meant as a compliment . . .

KATRINA

It wasn't taken as one.

ICHABOD

Think of it as no more than a simile, a metaphor . . .

KATRINA

I'll take it as good-bye, Master Crane. (*She runs out.*)

ICHABOD

But, Miss Katrina . . . Women. What's to please them? "As golden as pumpkin pie . . ." It doesn't seem offensive. Would a man take offense to such an expression? "Master Crane, your hair is as yellow as cider." Seems innocent enough to me. If she were not such a cook, such a thought would not occur, but a cook she is. Oh, Ichabod, build your good graces again. Will you miss her partridge pies with chestnuts, her roast tom turkey and clams, her taffy, her pies, her cheeses, her wines, her (*hearing the widow's muffled voice from beneath the boardwalk, he listens for a moment and ends hopefully*) . . . ducks? . . . No more. Well, to home, Master Crane . . . (*Ichabod starts offstage; Brom, hidden behind the tree, croaks like a frog. Ichabod stops, looks toward the origin of the sound, and pokes at it with his walking stick; he hears nothing. He starts off again, but his curiosity overcomes him and he returns to prod again with his stick. This time Brom responds with a croak. Ichabod tries to rouse the frog from its hiding place with his stick, jabbing it into the dark recesses among the tree roots. Brom seizes the end of Ichabod's stick and holds fast. Ichabod becomes increasingly alarmed and pulls frantically on the stick. Brom releases it; Ichabod tumbles down, gets up, and hurries off, but again he feels compelled to search out a natural explanation. He moves closer to the sound and pokes his stick around in the area where the sound originated. A boy creeps up behind Ichabod and pulls on his coattails. Ichabod freezes, then slowly turns around, but the boy stays directly behind him, out of sight. Ichabod stops, by now both perplexed and a little fright-*

ened. He pokes at the origin of the sound; the boy lifts Ichabod's hat from his head. Afraid to look around, Ichabod reaches up for his hat and finds nothing. The boy taps him on the shoulder and offers him the hat. Ichabod grabs it, claps it on his head, and tries to escape, but he is suddenly surrounded by all of the Sleepy Hollow Boys. He leaps in terror and, to his surprise, lands in Brom Bones's arms.)

BROM

Hello, Master Crane.

ICHABOD

Hello, Master Bones.

BROM

Master Van Brunt to you. (*Ichabod nods weakly.*) Gone a-courting, Master Crane?

ICHABOD

A bit of evening air, you know, exercise, good for the heart and liver.

BROM

With a young lady on your arm?

ICHABOD

Well, I . . . yes, Miss Katrina and I . . . that is, we met, accidentally, on the path and I . . . to escort her home, no more . . . dark paths, a gentleman's arm needed . . .

BROM

If Miss Katrina needs a man's arm, I'll be there.

ICHABOD

Oh. Yes, well, of course that's true, but then you weren't there, were you? And I felt that I couldn't abandon her, as it were, to the wilds of the woods.

BROM

Yes. Things happen in the woods, Master Crane.

ICHABOD

Oh. Do they?

BROM

Perhaps, Master Crane, it would be better for you to stay clear of the woods.

ICHABOD

In this vicinity?

BROM

Yes. They are particularly dangerous in the vicinity of Miss Katrina's, Master Crane.

ICHABOD

Well, I will, of course, remember that, and I thank you for your solicitous advice . . . (*Suddenly the sounds of a scuffle beneath the boardwalk are heard. The Sleepy Hollow Boys scatter, deserting Brom. Widow Winetraub is seen behind the ramp.*)

WIDOW

Think to terrorize a defenseless poor widow, do you? Out of my way, out of my way! Ah, Master Crane. Just in time!

ICHABOD

(*hurrying to help her onto the boardwalk*) Widow Winetraub!

WIDOW

Hunting for mushrooms. (*smacking Brom with her handbag*) You might be a gentleman, Master Bones!

BROM

Yes, ma'am.

WIDOW

My poor Hildy's mired in the mud. Give her a hand. (*She pushes Brom off the boardwalk, showing him where Hilda is.*) You'll come for strudel, Master Crane? (*She picks up her picnic basket.*)

ICHABOD

Strudel, Widow Winetraub?

WIDOW

It'll die of chills if you stand gaping much longer, Teacher. It's made to eat hot.

ICHABOD

(*offering her his arm*) By all means, Widow Winetraub.

WIDOW

Not that it'll matter to you and your stomach, but it's made by my daughter's own hand.

ICHABOD

A splendid girl, Widow. (*They exit. A feeble plea comes from Hilda as she pokes her head above the boardwalk.*)

HILDA

Ma? (*Blackout.*)

Scene v   Strudel and Gremlins

Ichabod and the widow are seated; Ichabod is just finishing a dish of strudel and cream, wiping his mouth with the napkin that is tucked under his chin.

ICHABOD

Splendid, splendid, splendid! I'm only sorry that I missed your charming daughter.

WIDOW

Well, she's a fool, Master Crane, and foolish besides, but a fine girl and a passable cook.

ICHABOD

More than passable, but . . . I must be off! Church in the morning (*kissing her hand*), Widow Winetraub.

WIDOW

(*giggling*) You're a terrible man, Teacher, terrible! (*Hilda appears at the door, tired and muddy.*) Hurry, girl, there's dishes to wash. You'll come again, Master Crane?

ICHABOD

When I smell the smell of strudel in the air, I'll be here before it's cool. Adieu, Widow Winetraub. (*He bows and leaves.*)

WIDOW

Hilda! Lollygagging in the mud! What's a poor widow to do? (*Blackout. The lights come up slightly; Ichabod is barely visible as he walks home from the widow's. The wind blows with an eerie sound. Suddenly, gremlins hop onto the stage and crowd around Ichabod, grabbing at his feet. They are shapeless little creatures with beards and bright red, glowing eyes. They continue to pester Ichabod, forcing him to flee. As he runs, he sings the Doxology to dispel his terror.*)

ICHABOD

> *Praise God, from whom all blessings flow:*
> *Praise Him, all creatures here below . . .*

(*He runs out.*)

Scene vi   Sunday Courting

Warm light floods the stage as Ichabod is immediately forced back onstage by members of the Sunday congregation who are singing the Doxology. Ichabod quickly composes himself and joins in the singing.

ALL

> *Praise Him above, ye heavenly host:*
> *Praise Father, Son, and Holy Ghost.*
> *Amen.*

(*By the end of the song the congregation fills the stage, facing the pastor, who stands at upstage left. All bow their heads, and the pastor reads the final benediction.*)

PASTOR

And on this eve of Halloween, may the Lord protect, may the Lord make his countenance to shine down upon you and give you peace. Amen. (*The people of the congregation chat with each other as they go out; the young girls immediately cluster around Ichabod. He flirts with all simultaneously, leading them out into the fall morning.*)

ICHABOD

I counted fourteen orioles and a partridge by a tree. Oh! The season of the grape! And a sweet for a sweet. (*He pops a grape in one girl's mouth, then offers grapes to others.*) And you and you and you. (*They all giggle. Brom and the Sleepy Hollow Boys glare at Ichabod as he reads the epitaphs in the church graveyard.*) Ah, yes. Tombstones. An education for the curious . . . shall we? "Here lies the earthly remains of Jan Van Ruyder, frightened to death by the Headless Rider." (*Surprised at the inscription, the girls all giggle, but a brief chill passes through Ichabod. He laughs.*) "Beneath this stone you read from lies one who reads no more." (*They all laugh. Ichabod spies Katrina and excuses himself from the bevy. The girls laugh and descend upon the Sleepy Hollow Boys. All exit but Ichabod, Katrina, and Brom, who lurks in a dark corner, angry and jealous.*) A fine fall morning!

KATRINA

It is, Master Crane. (*She flirts with Ichabod to tease Brom.*)

ICHABOD

I hope that I'm forgiven for the night past.

KATRINA

You are.

ICHABOD

May I be so bold as to come again soon?

KATRINA

You may do me better. You may escort me now. (*They pass directly in front of Brom as they leave.*)

ICHABOD

Could I say that I am honored and do it justice? Could I say that I am pleased and speak half of my joy? Miss Katrina, I am the luckiest man in the Hollow this Sunday morning! (*Pause. Brom whistles. The Sleepy Hollow Boys immediately appear and cluster around him. He whispers his orders, and the boys go off laughing. Brom lingers a moment longer behind Ichabod and Katrina.*)

BROM

The luckiest man, Master Crane? (*He laughs and exits on one side of the stage as Katrina and Ichabod enter from the other and sit on a bench on the ramp. Katrina carries a dulcimer.*)

ICHABOD

Delicious meal, Miss Katrina. Shadows fall very early.

KATRINA

Halloween night, Master Crane.

ICHABOD

(*trying to sound lighthearted*) Oh, yes, Halloween. A tune, Miss Katrina? (*She smiles and strums the dulcimer.*) In honor of the season, our golden harvest, our plentiful prospects. (*He recites as if giving a dramatic reading.*)

      Onions, grapes, and watermelon,

      Salted beef and scarlet plums,

      Baskets full of shining apples . . .

(*The Sleepy Hollow Boys make strange noises — low moans and squeals. Ichabod hears the mysterious sounds. He stops; his eyes move in the direction of the sounds. He sees Katrina looking at him; he smiles as if it is nothing and goes on, but his recitation lacks conviction. He listens carefully now.*)

      Tables crowned with sparkling rum . . .

(*There is another noise, this time on the opposite side of the stage. After an uncomfortable pause Ichabod smiles.*)

      Radishes and carrots glowing,

      Golden rye and Indian corn . . .

(*Brom can be seen in his hiding place under the ramp. He speaks to Ichabod, creating an echo effect.*)

BROM

> Ichabod Crane . . . Crane . . . Crane . . .

ICHABOD

> (*after a pause, tensely*) Your father's out walking?

KATRINA

> (*knowing immediately that it was Brom who called Ichabod's name*) Oh, no, sir, always a pipe after supper, by the fireplace.

ICHABOD

> By the . . . Yes. I thought . . . the wind. No more. (*He resumes his recitation.*)
>
> > Wine for drinking, jam for spreading . . .

SLEEPY HOLLOW BOY

> (*in a ghostly, echoing voice*) Ichabod. (*All the Sleepy Hollow Boys echo "Ichabod . . . 'bod . . . 'bod . . ."*)

ICHABOD

> You're sure that . . . ?

KATRINA

> Oh, yes, sir, sure of it.

ICHABOD

> Your younger brother, sister . . .

KATRINA

> None, Master Crane.

ICHABOD

> (*edging toward the spot the noise came from*) A neighbor child likely . . .

KATRINA

> None, sir.

ICHABOD

> (*suddenly peering under the floorboards*) A-ha!

KATRINA

> Anything, Master Crane?

ICHABOD

> No, nothing, I thought . . . perhaps a mouse but . . . nothing. The wind. Yes. A storm brewing.

KATRINA

> It's very quiet out, Master Crane.

ICHABOD

Yes, you're . . . right.

SLEEPY HOLLOW BOYS

Yes, you're right.

ICHABOD

(*trying to be nonchalant*) Well! Time to be off. Long walk ahead and back.

KATRINA

You won't forget?

ICHABOD

The frolic? No, no, first there, last to leave . . .

BROM

Ichabod Crane . . . Crane . . . Crane . . .

ICHABOD

Nothing?

KATRINA

Nothing, Master Crane.

ICHABOD

Nothing. Yes. Of course. Absolutely nothing. Well! Time to be home.

SLEEPY HOLLOW BOY

Ich-a-bod Crane . . . (*All the Sleepy Hollow Boys echo the name.*) Ich-a-bod Crane . . .

ICHABOD

(*hurriedly leaving*) Yes. Nothing. Good day, Miss Van Tassel. Good luck. I hope . . . we'll meet again.

SLEEPY HOLLOW BOYS

(*standing up suddenly and shouting*) Ichabod! (*As Ichabod runs out, Brom laughs.*)

KATRINA

Brom Bones! (*He leaps onto the ramp and sits down beside her, laughing.*)

BROM

Miss Van Tassel!

KATRINA

You may excuse your acquaintances. (*Brom motions for the Sleepy*

Hollow Boys to disappear and they go out sullenly.) You've no call to plague Master Crane.

BROM

Master Crane is made to be plagued.

KATRINA

I hope you'll find another place to do it than on my porch.

BROM

Perhaps he won't come to your porch again.

KATRINA

He is invited tonight.

BROM

And am I?

KATRINA

(*pause*) It's the Halloween frolic; come masked. (*She starts to leave, sweeping past him.*)

BROM

(*catching her hand*) And my invitation? (*She pauses, rises on her toes, kisses him on the cheek, and exits. Brom laughs and exits singing "I'm just a lucky man . . .*")

Scene vii   Preparing for the Party

Ichabod enters from the right, whistling the song that Brom was singing. He is dressed for the frolic at Katrina's. He pantomimes looking in a mirror, facing left, getting his tie on straight.

ICHABOD

(*singing*) I'm just a lucky man . . .
(*He shouts to Van Ripper, who is offstage.*) Van Ripper!

VAN RIPPER

(*from offstage*) What?

ICHABOD

Is my horse prepared?

VAN RIPPER

(*still offstage*) What?

ICHABOD

Is my horse prepared?

VAN RIPPER

(*entering*) Gunpowder? There's a saddle on him. (*Ichabod laughs good-naturedly; nothing will upset him on this night.*)

ICHABOD

But is he groomed? Is the leather oiled?

VAN RIPPER

You put a brush to that broomtail and his mane'll come off. He's held together with dirt and meanness and no more.

ICHABOD

Never mind, never mind. Give him oats and corn, Master Van Ripper. Even his temper won't deter me. I'm off to Miss Katrina! (*He turns toward the tree at the side of the proscenium as if to get something out of a closet.*)

VAN RIPPER

(*going off to feed Gunpowder*) Hope you make it. Gunpowder don't see any too well with the sun gone down. Still, he's slow enough to lead if you have to . . .

ICHABOD

Good night, Van Ripper! (*Van Ripper exits. An actor-image of Ichabod appears across the stage from Ichabod, who walks back to the mirror. The actor copies Ichabod's movements and walks toward him. They face each other in a mirror-image pose. The sequence is carefully choreographed. Ichabod looks at his teeth, adjusts his clothes, and practices a dance; the actor-image reflects every motion. Ichabod turns away to get something, and the actor-image peers around the imaginary frame and makes a face. Ichabod catches this out of the corner of his eye, but when he turns around the actor-image reflects Ichabod's motions as before. Ichabod turns away again, and the actor-image, becoming grotesque and threatening, reaches for him. Ichabod turns and escapes offstage. Blackout.*)

Scene viii   The Van Tassels' Party

It is night, and Ichabod, still offstage, has arrived at the Van Tassels' stables. Faint sounds of music and laughter are heard from offstage in the direction of the party.

ICHABOD

(*offstage*) Easy, Gunpowder, easy, boy. There. That's your bag, boy, good rolled oats. (*He enters and suddenly several small masked figures dart out at him from the shadows and dance around him. The terrified Ichabod cries out, splutters, and whirls about, trying to escape them. Finally, as Cornwall takes off his mask, the stage lights intensify so that the figures are seen to be schoolboys in Halloween masks.*)

CORNWALL

(*taking off his mask*) Good evening, Master Crane.

ICHABOD

Oh, it's you, Cornwall. Just a mask. (*He laughs. The boys escort him to the party. As Ichabod and the boys leave, Widow Winetraub enters, flirting outrageously with Brom.*)

WIDOW

Master Brom, Master Brom, you are such a joker!

BROM

Only with such a lady.

WIDOW

Oh, I swan, Master Brom, a lady will be hard put to handle a man like you! (*The guests at the Van Tassels' party burst onto the stage, dancing.*)

BROM

We'll try that now, shall we, Widow? (*Brom whirls her into the dance. Ichabod and Katrina dance together and then are separated. Laughing, he tries to catch her, but the other dancers keep them apart. Finally, he catches her hand and they dance slowly together; Ichabod is in ecstasy. He turns Katrina in a graceful pirouette. The other dancers freeze. Ichabod, completing an intricate step of his own invention, turns back to see what he hopes will be Katrina's admiration, but instead he sees her lean toward Brom and gently kiss his cheek. The dance sweeps on. The Sleepy Hollow Boys threaten the dancers with jack-o-lanterns on poles, playfully frightening them. One of the boys holds a large jack-o-lantern over Ichabod's head. The dancers begin to swirl offstage and to drift homeward, waving their goodbyes. Ichabod tries to pretend indifference, a game loser. He and Katrina remain at the center; Brom begins to leave but lingers, waiting for Katrina. Ichabod, holding a giant jack-o-lantern, plays the fool a little in his disappointment.*)

ICHABOD

Alas, poor lantern, I know thee well, but one poor night to live, poor Halloween jack-o-lantern. (*He looks up and smiles at Katrina, but she averts her eyes.*)

KATRINA

I'm sorry, Ichabod.

ICHABOD

Oh, the pumpkin won't mind. It's the curse of his family to smile but one night . . . (*Katrina begins to cry. She is happy to have Brom but sad to hurt Ichabod. Ichabod helps her to talk about it.*) I know, I know . . .

KATRINA

I'm sorry, it's Brom.

ICHABOD

A singing master makes a poor husband.

KATRINA

And a practical joker a worse one. But he'll change, Ichabod, I know he will. He's still a boy and impetuous and rough and . . . and honest. Ichabod, I know he loves me.

ICHABOD

And I love . . . to eat! Well, Miss Katrina, I'll dance at your wedding.

KATRINA

Don't forget me altogether, Ichabod.

ICHABOD

I'll never forget your pies. (*She runs to join Brom. As they exit, Ichabod stands a moment wistfully watching them, then leaves.*)

Scene ix   The Ride of the Headless Horseman

The stage lighting creates the illusion of a murky night. Black velour curtains hang at the back of the stage. The amplified sounds of crickets, moaning wind, horses' hooves, and animals calling heighten the effect. Brom's voice calling "Ichabod! Ichabod!" echoes eerily in the night. Ichabod appears upstage, behind the platform. He wears a horse-body costume; the head is jointed so that it can bob up and down. Lighting and the motion of the actor create the appearance of a man riding a horse. A red light shines on Ichabod's back, and a giant tree branch claws at him. He hears Brom's voice and looks back in terror, urging the horse to go faster. The volume of Brom's voice and the hoofbeats mounts in a crescendo as a black cloth is flung over Ichabod's head.

The music crashes, and the scene ends in an abrupt blackout. Then a giant jack-o-lantern that fills the entire stage is created with lighting focused on portions of the set. Red light falls across the curved platform to form the mouth; triangular boxes containing lights behind red cloth are lowered at the back of the stage to form the eyes and the nose. This image is maintained for the length of a dissonant chord struck on the organ. Blackout.

Scene x   Finale

When the lights come up, it is the following morning. A jack-o-lantern and Ichabod's hat lie on the stage. Cornwall enters, sees the hat, and tries it on.

ICHABOD'S VOICE
   (*singing over an offstage microphone*)
      The Lord sings out . . .
   (*Cornwall removes the hat, and the voice stops. He puts the hat back on.*)
      The Lord sings . . .
   (*Cornwall removes the hat, and again the voice stops. He puts the hat on again. Gremlins like those that haunted Ichabod appear and chase Cornwall off the stage.*)

The Legend of Sleepy Hollow. ''There's no such things as ghosts . . . !''
(Photograph by Paul Corlette.)

The Legend of Sleepy Hollow. ''What trifle of gossip could possibly be so edifying and full of import . . . ?'' (Photograph by Don Yunker.)

Brom's Tale

(Tempo, rhythm, and meter are relative since this section is intended as an accompaniment to the text.)

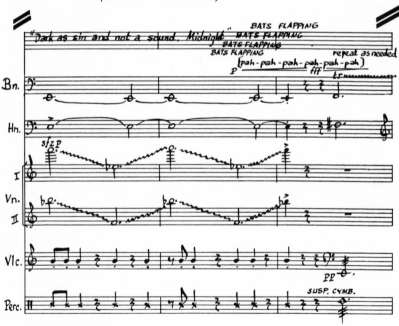

NOTE: Music for *The Legend of Sleepy Hollow* composed by Roberta Carlson.

✱ A lip technique (lip drop) common to the jazz idiom.

N.B. — A good addition to this section, if an electric organ is used, would be the use of the portamento bar, set at 4' and with some reverb, for moaning sounds.

Kidnapped in London

by Timothy Mason

Inspired by John Bennett's *Master Skylark*

CORIN

> *Believe me when I say,*
> *God makes with man a happy jest:*
> *The Fool — he knows the way,*
> *And the tawny bird who left his nest*
> *Sings now a shining lay.*
> *And you who watch are now twice-blest:*
> *You hear the song. Now walk the way.*

Kidnapped in London was first produced by the Children's Theatre Company of the Minneapolis Society of Fine Arts in January 1970. The script was edited by Linda Walsh Jenkins with the assistance of Carol K. Metz.

Cast of Characters

Corin Marvell
Benjamin Marvell
Nellie Marvell
Citizens, sailors, and
    tradesmen

Two rogues
Women and serving girls
Peasant man
Jailor and prisoners

THE PLAYERS OF BLACKFRIARS

Diccon Burbage
Fan-Dan
Cuthbert Bogs
Geoffrey Bile
Joseph Taylor
Apprentices and actors

Sequence of Scenes

Notes on the Play

Corin Marvell, a shepherd boy visiting Elizabethan London with his parents, is kidnapped by a group of actors, the Players of Blackfriars. Although Corin becomes the pet of London, he yearns to return home. When he is finally given the opportunity to do so, however, he realizes that he belongs in the theater. The play fashioned around this story is a rich blending of characters and scenes: London street vendors and a marketplace, sailors on shore leave, a tavern, a gloomy prison, and tantalizing bits from masques and tableaux of the Elizabethan theater. Ballads, vendors' cries, renaissance dances, and the full flavor of Elizabethan speech combine to recreate the musical color of the period.

The set resembles an open inn-yard theater, and it is constructed in such a way that the contemporary audience's relationship to the stage is the same as that of an Elizabethan audience behind the groundlings. A central revolving platform has gallery space on either side of it; each gallery has two levels. Tapestry curtains are hung from posts on the platform. Upstage of the platform is a balcony and a chamber for the use of the Players. The period costumes are made of velvet, silks, and homespun. The overall stage palette emphasizes golds, greens, and earthy colors.

Act I

Scene i   Dusk in the Warwickshire Hills

Corin is seated on a mound of hay. He sings softly in the dusk, accompanied by various evening sounds. Nellie calls from offstage.

NELLIE
    Cory! Whur beest thou? Come now. 'Tis gone bedtime, lad!
CORIN
    (*singing*)

        To Mary, Queen, awakening
        One bleak midwinter morn,
        Came like a falcon to its king,
        Fair Jesu to be born.

        And though the wind was cold as stars,
        And though the shadows, long,
        When winter's cage flung wide its bars
        The skylark found his song.

        For spring awoke that very day,
        And warmed December's dawn,

> *To hear the skylark's gladsome lay,*
> *Like dew upon the lawn.*

NELLIE

(*offstage*) Now, I says, Cory!

CORIN

> *To Mary, Queen, awakening*
> *One bleak midwinter morn,*
> *Came like a falcon to its king,*
> *Fair Jesu to be born.*

NELLIE

Cory! (*A frog croaks.*)

CORIN

(*laughing*) Sssssh! Do na thou sing so, old toad. Tch, tch, tch, such a croak! List' to thy bird friend here. He hath more grace . . .

NELLIE

(*offstage*) Corin! I've ears, ye know! I hear thee. Come in out o' that!

CORIN

(*imitating Nellie*) I've ears, ye know, Corin . . . Lambs and she-goats, soft now. Sing low. Mother shall come wroth wi' thee. She hath ears, ye know. (*He yawns and stretches.*) Stars and bright things — do na shine so loud. 'Tis gone bedtime, don't ye see.

BENJAMIN

(*entering and walking toward Corin*) Sloth and folly, Nell. I'll have no idler for a . . . Corin Marvell! I bid thee come, and come now, if thou wouldst go wi' me morrow to London town.

CORIN

I' faith, Father, I was not idle. I was minding the flock, sir, with an eye to that old ram, sir, do ye know the one, butting and jumping at whiles, sir, and may I na go wi' thee, Father, may I na?

BENJAMIN

Minding the flock with a silly song, and a man might earn his bread dancing in a motley jerkin, if ye'd have thy way. Ah, Corin, shun folly and do na let thy head be turned. Come now to bed. We've a long journey on the morrow. (*He leaves.*)

CORIN

(*to the hills*) My sheep and billies, go quiet now to sleep. Mind ye shun folly till I come back. I've a long journey on the morrow. (*Blackout.*)

Scene ii   London!

A sudden clash of tambourines is heard and the lights focus on downstage center, where a jester pops out from behind the platform curtain. He jerks like a puppet on strings and beckons to the audience to follow him. Young girls dance by. Shafts of dim light fall across the stage, allowing the audience brief glimpses of the people of the city who are gathered about; each character is frozen in position. The vendors slowly come to life, hawking their goods in a round.

FIRST VENDOR
    (*singing*)
        Red onions! Buy my onions!
SECOND VENDOR
    (*singing*)
        Fine laces for a lady!
THIRD VENDOR
    (*singing*)
        Fresh mackerel! Fresh mackerel!
FOURTH VENDOR
    (*singing*)
        New oysters! New oysters!
    (*The stage slowly comes to life as tradesmen, fine ladies and gentlemen, chimney sweeps, and others cross, call out, and dance.*

The pace accelerates until the stage becomes a swirl of intoxicating song and activity. Sailors are seen unloading a barge at downstage left. Corin enters, running. His parents follow, buying and haggling in the marketplace; they are ill at ease in the big city. The boy stops, smells the air, and looks about him as a sailor begins to sing. The vendors continue to hawk in the distance.)

FIRST SAILOR

(*singing*)

Cast her down easy, me hearty lads all,
Leave Gabriel *behind,*
For the goodliest mate that ever did sail
Sleeps now among the brine.

Full twenty and four at Whitsuntide,
Afore the moon did bleed,
Come into port on Michaelmas,
With only twenty-three.

There fast on deck stood gentle Dan,
Whilst we all hied to lee.
"Come down," I cried, "my Danly, dear,
Thou canst na still the sea."

"I'll hold the stays," sung darlin' Dan,
"Aye, with me hands blood-red.
'Tis but the wings of Gabriel
Beatin' 'bout my head.

"Tell me lady, Marilee,
How she lost her Dan —
On the good ship Gabriel,
True as any man."

Came the morning, still the storm,
Danly, he was gone.

In the deep — some angel's wings,
Driftin' with the foam.
(*Pause and quiet. Suddenly a sailor throws Corin up in the air and sets him on his shoulder.*) Ahoy, lads, here be a piece o' baggage! Do ye want it for to sail the briny deep?

SECOND SAILOR

Aye, that we do!

THIRD SAILOR

Need another hand!

SECOND SAILOR

I says, bring it along!

THIRD SAILOR

To Africa!

FIRST SAILOR

What, to Africa! To Ethiopia! Blackamoors!

SECOND SAILOR

Rings through their noses!

THIRD SAILOR

Bones!

FIRST SAILOR

What say ye, boy? Will ye have a bit o' the sailor's life?

BENJAMIN

(*from across the stage, where he and Nellie are shopping*) Cory! Hie thee here!

CORIN

(*to the sailors as they set him down*) Nay, sir. But thankee, sir. (*He runs to his parents.*)

NELLIE

(*taking Corin in her arms*) There's me stout son. Did yon rogue fright thee?

CORIN

Nay, Mother. But didst thou hear him sing? 'Twas the beautifullest thing ever I list' to. I' faith, he was singing about islands and he said that might be I could go there. (*Tambourine, drum roll, horn, and cymbals announce the Players of Blackfriars. They enter and*

swirl across the stage, tumbling and waving swords and banners.
The center platform turns, holding several actors, and the citizens
gather at the left on the upper and lower levels, laughing and
murmuring. Corin stands among those at the front of the crowd. In
a matter of moments the stage becomes full. The jester performs a
pantomime, and the other Players sing.)

PLAYERS

> *(singing)*

>> The hunt is up, the hunt is up,
>> And it is well nigh day:
>> And Harry, our king, has gone a-hunting,
>> To bring his deer to bay.

>> The east is bright with morning light
>> And darkness it is fled.
>> The early horn wakes up the morn,
>> To leave its idle bed.

>> The hunt is up, the hunt is up,
>> The dogs are running free.
>> The woods rejoice at the merry noise
>> Of "Hey, tan-ta-rah, ta-ree!"

A HERALD

> *(reading from a long scroll)*

>> Good, me citizens, hark ye well!
>> Today to 'friars come ye all,
>> Where performed anon shall be
>> Most gay and witty comedie!
>>> *The Dame's Displeasure*
>> Wherein a lady seeks to win
>> The attentions of two gentlemen.

(Fan-Dan and Bile do a comic pantomime, trying to win the favor
of a maiden, with Joseph as the maiden. There is a great deal of
interaction with the spectators throughout this scene. Burbage and
Bile perform a comic sword fight to finish the street presentation.)

FAN-DAN

(*pointing to Corin*) Here, Diccon, see how the bumpkin gapes!

BURBAGE

Why lad, thy mouth's so wide, could easy catch a cow! What? Hast thou no penny for the play? Take ye this one, then. (*He tosses Corin a coin.*) And, pray, shut thy mouth. (*In a friendly manner he taps Corin's mouth shut. The spectators laugh; the Players sing and walk away to find another audience. Corin turns to his parents, holding up the coin, but stops short when he hears his father.*)

BENJAMIN

Such a pack o' rogues! Puttin' folly an' proud notions into silly heads. Cory. Nell. Come. (*Benjamin and Nellie leave. Corin stands, torn between his desire to be obedient and his fascination with the actors. He looks toward the Players and then toward his parents. He looks at the coin and makes his decision. He runs after the actors.*)

Scene iii   Masque:
"A Wedding in the Glade"

The scene is the Blackfriars' afternoon performance. The performance is nearly finished; "A Wedding in the Glade" and the Epilogue remain. The members of the audience stand about; some are eating, a few hold up babies so that they can see, and others are leaning on the railings. Corin is among them. Actors holding arches of flowering branches stand on the revolving stage at upstage center. Others carrying wreaths of evergreens and blossoms are at downstage left and right. An actor costumed as the Old Man of the Woods enters. As he calls to the

various creatures in his poem, they enter in pairs from either side of the
stage and form a V opened toward the audience. The creatures are
identified by their masks as nymphs, unicorns, foxes, deer, and birds.

OLD MAN OF THE WOODS

> Come elves, sprites of earth and air,
> Secret spirits, nymphs, and bearded trolls;
> Snow-crowned unicorns — hie thee here and there
> With the Friends of Faerie to see married, merry souls.
> Humbler creatures, too, I summon thee;
> Little foxes, proud-head deer and fawn . . .
> Any other? Aye, there's two-legg'd Greybeard — me!
> Now a wedding dance dance ye on a crystal lawn.

(The creatures dance while the Bride and the Groom enter and
stand under the flowering arch. The Old Man of the Woods hands
each a wreath, and each crowns the other.)

> For in this holy grove beneath the bowers
> Are wed in secret, King and Queen of May;
> And in heart's secret place bloom secret flowers
> To lighten Lord and Lady's secret way.

> And who, dear friends, hath seen what no man dreams,
> But you, dear friends, in whom this secret gleams.

(The Bride and the Groom cross to downstage center and stand
with joined hands. As Burbage speaks, the Old Man of the Woods
stands behind the couple and slowly lifts his cape; it is lined in
gold, and it forms a golden backdrop for the couple.)

BURBAGE

> When next with fire and smoke yon sun of wonder
> By Ocean's lips devoured be, and put asunder
> Are all our fancies — all our dreams, like dreams,
> Forgot and vanished — then shall grow till seems
> Them waking visions, strange shapes of myst'ry and delight.
> These our simple phantoms change, take flight,
> And move men's souls. No longer one man's gesture,

Another's song, but alter'd so, a future
Age shall marvel, that sprung from these rough boards
A dance undying on ever-green greenswards.
(All join hands and dance a courtly masque, weaving in and out until finally the Bride and the Groom are framed at the center by creatures and flowers. The couple throws rose petals at the audience as the lights fade.)

Scene iv   Kidnapped!

The stage is empty except for Corin. He picks up rose petals scattered by the Players and lets them drift through his fingers. Dazed, he talks to himself.

CORIN

Oh. 'Twas good and . . . fine. I' faith, 'twas very good and fine. *(He does a few dance steps in imitation of what he has seen, then looks around and realizes that he is alone. He suddenly remembers that he has left his parents behind.)* Mother . . . my Father . . . *(People drift across the stage. A man and a woman walk by in conversation. Corin runs to them. He grabs the woman's arm and she whirls around.)* Mother! . . . oh, mum, I . . . *(The woman pulls away gently, and she and the man laugh as they exit.)*

WOMAN

He thought I was his mother! *(Other people pass by Corin, adding to his confusion and loneliness; some hurry across the stage carrying baskets. An old man and two drunks meander past. An elegant lady carrying a rose approaches Corin and he gapes in awe; she*

smiles and hands him the rose, then exits. Finally, he sits on the
edge of the stage at the center and, as one would whistle in the
dark, he begins to sing.)

CORIN

(*singing*)

>   To Mary, Queen, awakening,
>   One bleak midwinter morn,
>   Came like a falcon to its king,
>   Fair Jesu to be born.

(*Burbage and Bogs enter, walking and talking, on the platform.*
Bogs carries a large sack. They notice Corin, who continues to
sing. At the same time two young toughs notice Corin also. The
actors' interest in the boy grows as they see how he deals with
the rogues.)

>   And though the wind was cold as stars,
>   And though the shadows, long,
>   When winter's cage flung . . .

(*One rogue grabs Corin's shoulder. Thinking that it is his mother,*
Corin whirls toward the bullies.) Oh, Mother, I thought I'd
never . . .

FIRST ROGUE

Oh, "Mother," is it?

SECOND ROGUE

So your mother looks like a man, does she?

CORIN

Well, you don't, that's sure!

FIRST ROGUE

I fecks, Country Billy here, his mother's a cow, likely.

CORIN

What, did ye say thy brother's a sow? Well, what's life like in the
hog trough, lads?

SECOND ROGUE

Say, listen, what are ye doin' round here, anyways? You should be
back on the farm where ye came from.

CORIN

> (*with heavy sarcasm*) Funny ye should ask, good sow —
> ohh — sir. I just now seen performed most gay and witty comedie,
> *The Dame's Displeasure*. Did ye see it, perchance? Ohhh,
> nay? Well, the dancers, they danced so . . . (*As Corin dances,
> he boxes with his opponents, kicks them, and throws them to
> the ground, but the rogues eventually overpower him and draw
> knives. Just then Burbage and Bogs intervene and scatter the
> bullies.*)

BURBAGE

> Here, here. Thy footwork's wondrous fine, lad.

CORIN

> Thankee, sir. But I be lost and canna find them, me mother and
> father. Why, sir, thou it was gave me the penny for the play, but
> now I canna find them and I wish I had na come at all.

BURBAGE

> What? Was our play not to thy liking? Did not the Blackfriars nor
> Richard Burbage himself suit thy tastes?

CORIN

> Oh, nay, sir, nay. 'Twas all most very grand, sir, truly. But me
> mother and father, they do na live here in this big place, and they
> must needs go home to the sheep tonight — if I do na find them,
> e'en so, they must needs go home.

BURBAGE

> Hoo, now, such a fuss. Thy parents will come for thee in time.
> Come lad, what is thy name?

CORIN

> Corin Marvell, sir.

BURBAGE

> See, Cuthbert. Marvell's his name and so is he. Truly, Corin, a
> marvel.

CORIN

> Thou art kind, sir, and a gentleman as never I looked on. But I
> must go now. I must find them afore dark.

BURBAGE

> Nay, do not haste away. Thou canst stay here till thy parents find

thee, and act with the Players besides. Why, thou'lt be famous, Corin!

CORIN

Thankee, sir, and very elegant it sounds, sir, but me mother and father would have none o' that. They needs me. For the sheep, don't ye know. To home.

BURBAGE

Enough of prattle! Thou'lt stay! (*more gently*) Come, Cory, I'll send Bogs here to look for thy parents. I promise thee. But with such marvel-gifts as thine, ye ought to act.

CORIN

Nay, sir. Fare thee well.

BURBAGE

(*advancing on Corin*) By damn, boy, thou must! (*Corin tries to run away.*) Bogs! (*Bogs leaps up, catches Corin, and throws him into the sack, and the two actors carry the boy into the darkness. Blackout.*)

Act II

Scene i Corin Meets the Company

The Swan's Down Inn. Members of the company and others in the tavern are frozen in position — throwing dice, drinking, talking, playing games, singing, and playing musical instruments. Bile crouches with a sack pulled over him. As a man pulls the sack off, Bile stands up and says "Peep!" and the scene comes to life. A woman sings "Bonny Peggy Ramsey" to a friend. When she finishes, a group sings an improvised drinking song. During the song there is movement, a hum of voices, and occasional laughter. Burbage and Bogs enter with Corin in the sack slung over Bogs's shoulder. They set Corin down at the center and pull off the sack. There is sudden silence in the tavern as everyone stares at Corin.

BURBAGE

    Well? (*The crowd murmurs. Fan-Dan hands a mug to Corin, who starts to drink, stops, puts his finger in the ale, makes the sign of the cross on himself, then flicks ale at Burbage and throws the mug into Fan-Dan's face.*)

CORIN

    'Tis well? (*He turns about, challenging them all. All laugh and applaud.*)

BURBAGE

    Now, don't ye see why it is I had to bring him! His name is Corin Marvell — ain't he, though. He's from the hills — or so he says — but somewheres the country sun must have set fire to his tongue and the forest deer have taught him grace. "'Tis well" what, Master Marvell? These are not thy goats: here be thy new colleagues of Blackfriars.

CORIN

I'd rather have me goats. (*Burbage laughs. There are varied reactions from the company to Corin's tongue. The following comments from the people in the tavern overlap until Bile silences them: "Oh, he's a beauty!" "Fire? Oh, his tongue's on fire, sure!" "Aye, and it's forked as well!" "Goats! He can go back to his goats, I says!" "But such a beauty!"*)

BILE

(*silencing the crowd*) Here, cuckoos! (*to Corin*) So. Corin, is it? Well, my name is Geoffrey Bile, master of song and light aires. Hast thou a tongue, sweet? A mouth? Little teeth? (*Corin breaks away and leaps over a bench. Joseph, a young actor, has had his head in a bowl of pudding. Looking up, he sees that Corin is in trouble. As Corin jumps over the bench, Joseph rises and quickly guides him to a table. Other stage action freezes as the lights focus on the two boys.*)

JOSEPH

Pay them no heed, Corin. They'll come fond of thee, ye know.

CORIN

My mother and father are fond of me, too, and more, I daresay.

JOSEPH

Thy mother and father! Hast any brothers, Cory?

CORIN

Nay, nor sisters, neither.

JOSEPH

Well, Cory, thou hast no brother, and I have no mother, see? Then we'll be brothers, what Cory? (*He pokes Corin.*)

CORIN

(*poking him back*) First, brother, tell me thy name, brother, afore I make thy eye black, brother.

JOSEPH

I be Master Joseph Taylor, playactor of Blackfriars. And ye, sir? (*He steps back with dignity and bows.*)

CORIN

> (*bowing very ineptly*) Corin Marvell, the son of my father, sir, shepherd. (*Joseph pours ale for them both and they sit down. Burbage has approached the table unnoticed and is listening.*)

JOSEPH

> Was that a bow, or are there ants in thy pants? Oh, Cory, I'll teach thee how to bow, and how to fence, and how to kiss a lady's hand, and . . .

CORIN

> To fence? With swords?

JOSEPH

> With . . . rapiers!

CORIN

> Cowr!

JOSEPH

> And with me, thou'lt be one of Bile's boys and sing till . . .

CORIN

> Bile who?

JOSEPH

> (*laughing*) Why, Geoffrey Bile, Cory. That one there. With the face like a prune what's been kept in a box overlong. (*He mimics the singing master.*) Tut, my cuckoo — Bile talks thus — birdies, open thy mouths . . . (*He breaks off, laughing.*) Faith, Master Burbage will teach thee how to playact and soon . . .

CORIN

> Master Burbage! Nay, he hath stolt me away from me home and I hates him.

JOSEPH

> Corin! Do na speak so about thy betters. I' truth, I have hated Diccon Burbage, at whiles. But some say that he is the best playactor in all of England — some say, Cory, that he be the best playactor ever was. So. Work hard and soon thou'lt perform with me, what Cory? . . . Come, brother, because a man's a low rogue is nothing against his acting. (*Burbage, standing behind the boys, has been listening. Now he steps into the light and grabs Joseph's*

hair in a grip meant to seem playful but a bit menacing at the same time.)

BURBAGE

Upon my troth, Joey's right, boy. Now, aren't ye pleased Diccon Burbage is making a famous man of ye?

CORIN

Master Joey is very kind, sir, but I canna say I be pleased, sir, because of I'm not, sir, I'm not. (*Blackout.*)

Scene ii   Fan-Dan

The curtain is drawn shut at the front of the center platform. Several boys are talking quietly and rehearsing upstage. Fan-Dan and Corin are seated on stools at downstage center, playing a game. Fan-Dan writes his name on his hands, then plays hide-and-seek, opening and closing his palms swiftly and moving them around. Corin tries to see what is written on them; he makes guesses. Finally, Fan-Dan shows his hands to Corin.

FAN-DAN

That's it. Fan-Dan. Now you've got it. Me name. See? Fan-Danny. Well . . . ? God's lid, boy! Gape and stretch! How do they call thee?

CORIN

Sir?

FAN-DAN

Thy name, block, what do they call thee? (*He slaps his hands on his knees in a playful rhythm.*)

CORIN

> (*imitating Fan-Dan and slapping his own knees*) THEY do na call me nothin', sir, because of I do na know THEM.

FAN-DAN

> Thy tongue's sharp anyways, Master Nothin', if thy wit's not. But they'll know ye soon enough, and ye them, I trow. They're a lot, they are. I remember . . .

CORIN

> Me mother an' father, they call me Cory. But that's not me name, Christian.

FAN-DAN

> Aye, they're a lot, sure. (*Fan-Dan does not hear well.*) "Colley," did ye say?

CORIN

> No.

FAN-DAN

> Well, Colley, just you take me own name, if they ain't a lot.

CORIN

> Robin, who's me cousin, says just "Cor" sŏmetimes.

FAN-DAN

> Well, Robin . . . (*Corin tries to tell him his name is not Robin.*) When it was I come to London, 'twas not me name at all. Did I na tell thee just now that me name is Fan-Dan?

CORIN

> Yes.

FAN-DAN

> Well, Colley, that was not me name at all.

CORIN

> What was it, then?

FAN-DAN

> Hired out here at the 'friars as 'prentice. Was not a bit older than ye are now, not a jot. And if they ain't a lot now, they were then, I'll tell you. "Foot it, Dan," they'd say, meaning to step it in the dance. I danced in those days, Colley-boy. "That's me Fan-Dan!" they'd say, "That's me pretty Danny-high-stepper!" From the first day, that's what they called me, don't ye see.

CORIN

Sir, pray, what was thy name?

FAN-DAN

I do na know why they said it. But they're a lot. 'Twas not me name. Fan-Dan. I told them they had it all wrong, but they just laughed and said it anyways. In faith, it's not me name. Me name is John. John Fish. (*Corin takes the pen and scribbles on his hand. He briefly repeats the hand game, then holds his palm open to Fan-Dan.*)

CORIN

Corin Marvell, John. Pleased.

Scene iii   Bile's Boys

As Corin and Fan-Dan end their game, Bile enters and the quiet stage suddenly bustles with activity. Joseph runs past Bile and catches a plumed cap that is thrown from the wings. Corin leaps up and rushes after Joseph; Bile's boys fill the stage, shouting and playing "keep away" with the cap. Bile is in the center of it all.

BILE

(*sputtering and using his stick on every boy within reach*) Point and counterpoint, cuckoo! Here, dreadful children. I loathe each and every one of ye. Little tarts, I'll do something to you. Ooohh, such nasties. What? Would ye tread on my toe? (*He holds his toe out for viewing.*) That same toe which was once much talked about in some very high places? (*A boy running by treads on the toe again.*) Ooohh! I shall put sharp things in thy shoes. I'll put cuckoos in sacks. You there, thou canst not tell a fugue from a fig!

Here, I'll staccato you! (*He flails at the boys with a stick. Suddenly Burbage enters. Bile straightens himself, mumbles, and acts stern. Burbage laughs a bit, then becomes stern himself.*)

BURBAGE

Peace, my little bucks! (*He throws his poniard into the stage floor, where it sticks, quivering. Instant silence. The boys group themselves into their choir positions quickly — all but Corin, who sits on the floor, convulsed with laughter, pointing at Bile's wig, which has slipped down around his shoulders.*) Thou, Marvell, in particular, had best heed me. Sir Geoffrey has told me . . .

BILE

Master of song, cuckoo, and light aires . . .

BURBAGE

Bile here has told me that thou spendest thy weeks moping for thy mother like a lost dog.

CORIN

Not lost, sir, but stolen.

BURBAGE

Wretched ingrate! Don't you know that thou'rt Blackfriars' favorite? The whole town's mad for thee! (*The other boys turn upstage, and Bile leads them in humming a soft madrigal.*)

CORIN

I was famous once. Famous wi' me mother an' father. Aye, famous.

BURBAGE

Listen, I do love thee. And I'll send thee home straightaway, if only ye'll act for me a bit longer. In faith, thou wert born to it, lad. Thou must. Yes, Corin?

CORIN

If I must, sir.

BURBAGE

That's my marvel-throat! (*to Bile*) Here, old prune-face, get these rogues out of here. And do please put that wig back on. (*Bile and the boys hurry offstage. Burbage calls back Corin and Joseph.*) Joey Taylor! Master Marvell! I did na give thee leave to go. Dost think, Master Marvell, that because ye can turn a fancy note or two that thou canst playact? Why, ye cannot even talk proper! Joey, show me that thou hast taught this boy to fence! (*Joseph and Corin take dueling swords and begin to fence. Corin does quite well, but Joseph is obviously better. Burbage shouts advice and encouragement. Joseph scores a touch.*) Come, give me thy weapon. (*Burbage fences with Joseph. Burbage's fencing is superior, and Joseph's sword falls to the floor.*) Well, no matter, boys. Ye've done me proud and proud I am. Corin, I shall grant thee thy wish.

CORIN

What, Master Burbage, thou'lt let me go home?

BURBAGE

Nay, now I did na say that. Nay, I grant thee today the master's part in the revel of spring! Thou'lt take the part of the young shepherd. I' faith, should suit thee well!

Scene iv   Masque: "A Tale of Spring"

The scene is backstage before the Blackfriars' performance. The boys don choir robes and practice bits of song. Bile clucks about, giving directions. Meanwhile the actors in the masque are getting into their costumes. Then Bile hurries the boys out. Blackout. The lights come up on an audience gathered in the orchestra pit; a chorus of boys on an upper level sings through the verses once before the tableau. As the chorus sings, a tableau is enacted with Corin as a shepherd; other boys play the roles of the maiden, a lamb, the rival suitor, the sun, and the moon. It is a simple tale of spring love, summer marriage, and autumn sorrow. The audience responds with "oohs" and "ahhs" and comments to the various actors.

CHORUS

   (*singing*)

      Two songs only does the lover sing:
      One for summer, one for spring.
      Let fail other seasons, other songs —
      'Tis not for these the lover longs.

      Two voices stir within the heart:
      One for dreams and one to part
      The soul from dreamings — pass them by;
      Other voices — let them die.

      In a glade, on a day,
      In the dreaming month of May,
      Lies our tale of love and lover —
      Tale of spring, tale of summer.

CORIN

   (*singing*)

      Fast alone the shepherd lives;
      The nightingale small comfort gives
      When even' falls and lambs do sleep,
      And no one grieves to hear me weep.

      One I know and her I'll woo,
      And for her hand in marriage sue.
      When even' falls and lambs will sleep,
      I'll comfort know and no more weep.

BOY SOPRANO

   (*singing*)

      In the shade, in the gloom,
      Of the waking month of June,
      Lies our tale of love and lover —
      Tale of spring, tale of summer.

  (*Pantomime: Courtship and marriage.*)

CORIN

(*singing*)

Summer came and I was wed,
And for a season round our bed
Did posies grow and myrtle bloom,
For joy that slept 'twixt bride and groom.

(*During the next stanza the rival suitor steals the bride.*)

The nightingale, never heeding
Flow'rs ripen, bursting, bleeding,
Sang of season's passing lover:
Tale of spring, tale of summer.

(*Pantomime: Corin draws a dagger and stabs himself while the audience calls to him not to do it. Flowers and laurels are thrown from the audience. The actors make a curtain call as the audience cheers. Corin is borne away on the arms of members of the audience. When the crowd has dispersed, Burbage is seen standing alone on the stage, his head sunk on his chest. The lights fade on him.*)

Act III

Scene i   "Two voices stir
within the heart . . ."

Burbage is alone, talking to himself and drinking from a goblet of cut glass.

BURBAGE

   (*singing*)

> *Two voices stir within the heart:*
> *One for dreams and one to part*
> *The soul from dreamings . . .*

(*speaking*) Nay, but from this one dream I would na fain be parted. He's the very spit o' meself, he is. What is it then, Burbage, twenty? Nay, thirty years since 'twas thou decked out in shepherd's garb for the revel of spring. My robes were not so fine as his, nor was our house as grand, for we had neither the Queen's grace nor even a Queen. For a roof, we had the sky — them damn birds kept after droppin' on us. I recall me once how a droppin' lit on little Jem's head. He just looked up, quick as ye please, and said, "Are the angels fartin' stars, now?" (*He pauses, lost in reverie.*) For a crowd, we had the rag-taggle o' London, but they loved us — loved me, even then. Oh, 'twas a heady wine. Went straight to me head and it was all I ever wanted. (*He snaps back to his present concern over Corin.*) But this Corin, now, this Marvell that I found — him I do not understand. No rag-tag he plays for, but lords and high dames. They sigh and wring their hands and throw flowers, plenty. Who wouldn't, with him stepping pretty as

130

ye please, speaking honey from out his throat? But once he's off, aye, the moment he steps down from the boards, it's all hills and billy-goats with him . . . But come, Diccon, dost understand thyself? Ye knew the hills, once . . . Aye. And I wonder, do the horses still sleep standin' up? And what of the Avon? . . . Fool, of course they do — been sleeping so since the seventh day. And the Avon — it flows. (*Again his thoughts drift to his own boyhood.*) What might ye have done in the hills, Diccon, if ye'd had the chance? . . . (*Heatedly he defends his choice.*) I made me own hills right here on these boards, I did; *and* loud streams *and* prancing fillies, and aught else I wanted. (*He argues with himself.*) Give the boy his chance, Diccon — his choice. Thou hast plenty other players — there's young Joe Taylor . . . (*He makes his decision.*) But the boy's the very spit o' meself. I canna let him go. Oh, these voices . . . (*He sings.*)

   . . . *pass them by;*
   Other voices — let them die.

(*Corin enters. Burbage calls him over and kneels to be at eye level with him.*) Cory, come here one time. Look at this piece of glass and tell me what thou seest.

CORIN

A goblet, Diccon. 'Tis thy goblet.

BURBAGE

Nay, but lad — look in the glass and what dost thou see?

CORIN

Me own face, many times.

BURBAGE

Hast ever seen the sun, Cory?

CORIN

O' course I have.

BURBAGE

What? Canst thou look in the sun, then, boy? Is it not too hot for thine eyes?

CORIN

Well, aye, sir, in faith it is too bright. I canna bear to see it. But when I turn like this wi' both eyes tight shut, I can feel it warm inside 'em.

BURBAGE

Good. Now, look ye at Diccon Burbage's eyes.

CORIN

They're blue.

BURBAGE

Remember the glass, boy.

CORIN

Me own face, twice.

BURBAGE

Oh, Corin, if ever thou canst bear to open thine eyes to the sun, thou'lt see thine own face, gazing back. (*The lights slowly fade out.*)

Scene ii   The Warwickshire Hills

Benjamin and Nellie converse with a gossipy peasant man at their cottage.

PEASANT

Lost? Far from it, nor dead neither! I' faith, I was there, see? 'Tis me custom, don't ye know, to go to London town come May Day. Soul o' man, nigh on ev'ry spring sincet I were a little nip I've made the journey, sure. I've kin there, don't ye know, in a big . . .

BENJAMIN

Come, man! Have done with the chatter! If he be not dead, then what?

PEASANT

Dead? Far from it, nor lost neither!

NELLIE

Lord be praised! Then what, then . . .

PEASANT

Why, thy son's famous, Ben. A playactor, don't ye know!

NELLIE

No! Famous, Ben!

PEASANT

Sings like a very angel. Blackfriars' favorite and the pet of all London.

NELLIE

Sings? What, did he sing then? We would sing together, at whiles, come Sabbath. I' faith, I taught him to sing, sure.

PEASANT

See, I was there meself. 'Tis my custom . . . (*He continues to mumble about himself.*)

NELLIE

Oh, Ben! We must fetch our son.

BENJAMIN

(*softly to himself*) Singing. Pet o' London. (*to Nellie*) Son? What son is that? In truth, I had a son. But this man here speaks of a playactor what's got famous. Whose son is that? (*to himself, over Nellie's lines*) Had a son. Boy was good wi' the sheeps. But whose son is that? That's not Ben Marvell's son . . .

NELLIE

(*under Benjamin's lines*) Our son. He canna be happy where he is at. Our son. Me own son. (*Blackout.*)

Scene iii   Escape!

*The Swan's Down Inn. The Players of Blackfriars and others in the
tavern are frozen as before in various positions: throwing dice, playing
other games, drinking, talking, singing, and playing musical instruments. As the lights come up, music propels the actors into motion. The
company is rowdy. Burbage is once again dicing with Bogs. Corin and
Joseph are at a separate table.*

AN ACTOR

> Come, Bile, what say ye to another round? (*He whistles for
> drinks.*)

BILE

> (*giggling, already a bit tipsy*) Oh, my cuckoo! 'Twould na be
> seeming. Still, my little nasties hath put me in ill humor. P'r'aps
> just one more.

AN ACTOR

> That's me bucko. What there — a jug of sack for Bile's nasties!

BILE

> What jug, silly. A barrel-full, cuckoo!

A WOMAN

> Oh, Geoffrey, thou'rt too scandalous!

BILE

> There comes a time, dear lady, when a man must drown discord.
> Here's to harmony! (*They drink, their arms interlocked.*) Wet.
> Wet. (*He giggles. The activity on the stage freezes. The lights
> focus on Corin and Joseph.*)

JOSEPH

> Nay! Run away, Cory? Thou canst not! Cuthbert Bogs there
> would stop thee straightaway.

CORIN

I care not a fig for Cuthbert Bogs, nor Diccon Burbage. I shall run!

JOSEPH

And wouldst thou leave me, as well?

CORIN

Joey, come with me! (*A lute softly plays "To Mary, Queen, Awakening."*) Thou'd love the hills, I know it. There's no fencing, but there's fishing. Fishes big as me, Joey . . . i' faith, bigger! (*The stage action resumes as Burbage swears.*)

BURBAGE

God's blood! (*The music stops.*) The bloody things canna always fall so! (*The company is hushed. Conversations gradually resume, then the action freezes again. Soft music is heard.*)

CORIN

The Warwickshire Hills in spring, Joey. And sometimes — there's a special place by the river's edge, see — and sometimes I sit there and sing, or, p'r'aps, just sit there . . . And once I found a bird there, Joey — just a little snip of a bird — too young to be out and about by hisself. I tried to make him go back to his nest, but he wouldn't, not him. So we just sang there, together, him and me — just sang. Oh, will ye na come, Joey? Will ye na?

JOSEPH

Nay, Corin, I will na. I canna, Cory. This is where I live, see? — These people, this . . . and I must live it. Must, brother. 'Tis very pretty to sing with a bird, Cory, I do na say it's not. But to sing for people — real persons, Cory — now that's something different altogether. It changeth them somehows, if ye know what I mean. But, I expect ye don't, what, Cory? That's something ye've to learn for thyself. (*The music stops and the stage action resumes.*)

BURBAGE

A plague on the dice! Bogs, if ye do not play me true, I swear I shall play thee on the end of my dagger!

BOGS

I canna answer for thy own ill fortune, sweetheart! (*The stage action freezes. Music.*)

CORIN

Then thou will na come with me?

JOSEPH

Nay, I will na.

CORIN

Will ye not even help me to escape?

JOSEPH

Aye, Cory, I shall . . . but sadly, Corin. (*The stage action resumes in slow motion.*) I'll see to Master Bogs, there, whilst ye leave. Fare ye well, Marvell.

CORIN

Good-bye, Joey. (*The music stops. The stage action resumes its normal tempo. Joseph swaggers past Bogs and Burbage.*)

JOSEPH

Why, Cuthbert Bogs, thou'rt a sight tonight — indeed thou art. (*Joseph jostles Bogs's mug of ale.*) Oh, look. Ye've spilled thy ale all down thy hose. Tut, tut. (*Bogs rises, angrily brushing off the ale. Bogs sees Corin heading for the door and shouts after him.*)

BOGS

Marvell! (*Burbage leaps up to chase Corin but is blocked by Joseph.*)

BURBAGE

Fool. (*He strikes Joseph. The crowd enters into the action, and chaos ensues. Joseph rises from the floor and struggles with Burbage.*)

JOSEPH

Cory, run! (*Burbage draws his poniard and wounds Joseph in the struggle. Corin runs back into the fray, places himself between Burbage and Joseph, and strikes Burbage.*)

CORIN

Do not touch him again, thou rogue! (*There is a moment's silence. Burbage sinks onto a bench, his hands covering his face. With a rush the crowd gathers around the wounded boy. Corin holds Joseph as the lights go out, and the music drops to a minor key.*)

Scene iv   In the Prison

The prison is dimly lit; tattered, emaciated men are seen behind gaping holes covered with bars. Some are chained to pillars; others wearing chains lie on the floor. Low moans are heard. A heavy door opens and a shaft of white light pierces the gloom. The jailor ushers in Corin and points the way. Corin sees Burbage at the center, his leg chained to the floor.

BURBAGE
  How is it with the boy?
CORIN
  He'll mend.
BURBAGE
  Thank God. And thank God ye came. Ye must hate me so; why come ye?
CORIN
  Ye sent for me and I came. If ye've naught else to say, I'll leave again. Good-bye.
BURBAGE
  Nay, Corin, dear heart. Do na leave just yet. I do na seek thy forgiveness, lad. I could not ask it. But I do have somewhat to tell thee. (*Jeers, moans, and rattlings are heard from the neighboring cells.*) Be still, dogs! (*He is in anguish over the prisoners' jeers.*) I set thee free, Corin. I am 'prisoned now for a time, as I have 'prisoned thee. I am bound, and thou art free and canst go home to thy house . . . and thou canst go . . . to thy house . . . I was mad, Corin, the dice made me so, I swear it. I did love thee, lad; dost truly hate me? Say thou dost not hate Diccon Burbage, Corin, please!

JAILOR

Move it, block. Time to go.

BURBAGE

Oh, Corin, dost remember when I found thee? Thou wert singing. Thou'rt no more bound to sing, but I fain would hear thee once more.

CORIN

(*after some hesitation*) I'll sing for thee, Diccon.

To Mary, Queen, awakening,
One bleak midwinter morn,
Came like a falcon to its king,
Fair Jesu to be born.

(*The prisoners shout for quiet.*)

JAILOR

Here, be still!

CORIN

(*singing*)

And though the wind was cold as stars,
And though the shadows, long,
When winter's cage flung wide its bars
The skylark found its song.

(*There is silence in the prison. Faces peer out at the boy.*)

For spring awoke that very day
And warmed December's dawn,
To hear the skylark's gladsome lay,
Like dew upon the lawn.

To Mary, Queen, awakening,
One bleak midwinter morn,
Came like a falcon to its king,
Fair Jesu to be born.

(*Silence. Corin looks around in wonder.*)

A PRISONER

Mea culpa, mea culpa, mea maxima culpa. Ideo precor beatam Mariam . . .

JAILOR

Time's good and up, sirs.

BURBAGE

My Marvell . . .

CORIN

I must be going, Master Burbage. (*Corin quickly kisses Burbage's hand on the bars and leaves.*)

PRISONER

. . . et te, Pater, orare pro me ad Dominum nostrum. (*The lights fade.*)

Scene v   Freedom!

Corin is alone on the Blackfriars' stage. The center platform curtains are closed behind him. He rummages through his old leather bag and pulls out his shepherd's clothes. He stands looking at them. One of the child-actors rushes past, half in and half out of his costume, and shouts to Corin.

BOY

Hurry, Cory! They're about to start! Get dressed, man!

CORIN

(*shouting after the boy*) Nay, Barry! I'm na coming at all. I'm leaving! I be free! (*The boy is gone before Corin has finished. Alone again, Corin continues to speak.*) I be free. (*He pulls on his old sheepskin cloak.*) Goin' home. To me home. (*Fan-Dan enters carrying a deer-head mask.*)

FAN-DAN

Time, gentlemen, please! Time! (*He sees Corin.*) Colley! Will ye foot it, kindly! Move, sir!

CORIN

Nay, Fan-Dan, I'm leavin' now, see? Goin' home to the hills.

FAN-DAN

Oh. I see. Well, good-bye, then.

CORIN

Good-bye.

FAN-DAN

But Colley, will ye remember to step high today in the dance. Be a high-stepper, Colley, not like some old cow, what?

CORIN

But Fan-Dan, I'm not . . .

FAN-DAN

I know, faith, I know ye can do it. I've seen ye. High-stepper like old Fan-Danny, that's it. Foot it, now! (*Fan-Dan exits. Corin lets the clothes drop from his hands; he stands, lost in reverie. An intense white light focuses on him. He bows, looks up, and shuts his eyes, then opens them, looks up again, and smiles.*)

CORIN

"If ever thou canst bear to open thine eyes and look at the sun . . ." (*Joseph enters; his wound is still bandaged.*)

JOSEPH

Come, Cory, what did Burbage say?

CORIN

He freed me. He said that I am no more bound to sing. He said that I may go home to the hills.

JOSEPH

Then, brother, I bid thee farewell and wish thee all godspeed. (*He bows formally. Corin lifts him up again.*)

CORIN

Nay, I shall na go. Now I am free, I would na be so. I canna go home, for this be my home. We'll be brothers a bit longer, what, friend? (*They look at each other in silence, then laugh. Blackout. The lights come up again immediately to reveal the company in tableau on the turning center platform. It stops as all face the center. An audience is gathered on either side of the stage on the*

upper and lower levels. It is the conclusion of the afternoon's
performance. Corin speaks the Epilogue.)

> Believe me when I say,
> God makes with man a happy jest:
> The Fool — he knows the way,
> And the tawny bird who left his nest
> Sings now a shining lay.
> And you who watch are now twice-blest:
> You hear the song. Now walk the way.

(He bows amid a shower of rose petals. The audience cheers as the
lights fade.)

Kidnapped in London. "I danced in those days, Colley-boy. 'That's me Fan-Dan!'
they'd say, 'That's me pretty Danny-high-stepper!'"
(Photograph by C. T. Hartwell.)

A Christmas Carol. "It's evening, sir . . . Christmas evening, sir."
(Photograph by Don Yunker.)

Kidnapped in London. "Run, Cory, fly!" (Photograph by C. T. Hartwell.)

Robin Hood: A Story of the Forest. "What was that you were saying about my mother?" (Photograph by Bruce Goldstein.)

The Legend of Sleepy Hollow. "The neighborhood abounds with tales, twilight superstitions, haunted spots." (Photograph by Paul Corlette.)

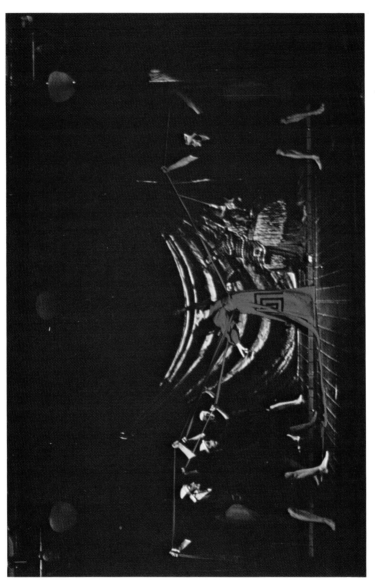

Sleeping Beauty. The Ogress, transformed into a giant spider, royally commands the center of the stage in front of a huge golden web. (Photograph by Gary Sherman.)

Robin Hood: A Story of the Forest

by Timothy Mason

ALAN-A-DALE

> *The king is coming, we light the pyre.*
> *The bloom of summer's love feeds the fire,*
> *The blood of autumn is gilding the flame*
> *And winter's chill is fled for shame.*
>
> *For shame is none of our lot cast.*
> *We seek the dawn and recall the past.*
> *The heart of lion, brave Richard's reign —*
> *Our lion-hearted, he's coming again.*

Robin Hood was first produced by the Children's Theatre Company of the Minneapolis Society of Fine Arts in October 1971. The script was edited by Linda Walsh Jenkins with the assistance of Carol K. Metz.

Cast of Characters

Ellen-a-Dale
Alan-a-Dale
Sheriff of Nottingham
Sheriff's men
Abbot
Maureen
Townspeople
Robin Hood
Friar Tuck
Much the Miller's son

Will Scarlet
Bob Smith
Peasant
Little John
Marion
OTHERS IN ROBIN'S BAND
    Ellis, Hob, Jon, Harry, Tom, Derry, Hugh, Peterkin, Julian, Frank, Ron, Eleanor, and about ten other men, women, and children who are not identified by name

Sequence of Scenes

Notes on the Play

Around the middle of the thirteenth century, somewhere in the East Midlands of Great Britain, men and women who had defied corrupt authority were declared outlaws by a wicked regent while their rightful king, Richard the Lion-Hearted, was away with the Holy Crusades. It was said that they lived in a forest called Sherwood and that when the snows came they lived in the caves that honeycombed the ground beneath the forest. This adaptation of the Robin Hood legend focuses on the life-style of the outlaws who built and maintained their community through the ritualistic power of song, dance, and the hunt. The "adventures" are internalized; the conflicts exist between the harsh wilderness environment and the personal struggles of men, women, and children who have been forced to create a new society outside the law.

A naturalistic forest setting is used for the entire play; it includes a grassy hillside with trees, exposed tree roots, and a stream with a log bridge. The palette of the set and the costumes is green, brown, gold, and black, and the textures of the construction materials emphasize the ruggedness of the environment.

Prologue

It is a summer's day several years before the action of the play begins. A harp pluck is heard; its sound carries the audience into the removes of fantasy and forest. A distant hunting horn is heard. From the darkness the cries of men, women, and children mingle with the barking of dogs. The horn sounds again, closer. Then the shouts and laughter fade into silence. With a sudden sharp crescendo of tambourine and drum, the lights come up on a rough platform and a ragged little pavilion. Beneath the pavilion a man drums while a woman dances. Men, women, and children sprawl about, eating and drinking, as they rest for a time on their way to a fair. People pass by carrying baskets and babies. Some watch the dancing. They are dressed in motley — greens, browns, and gold — the colors of the forest. The Sheriff's men lounge about, the blacks and grays of their uniforms contrasting sharply with the colors worn by the other folk. The Sheriff and the Abbot, resplendent in brightly colored cloaks and costumes of expensive fabrics, sit at the center and watch the dancing woman, Ellen-a-Dale. She finishes her dance and passes a mug for coins amid applause and laughter.

SHERIFF

(*to Ellen-a-Dale*) What's your name? (*She does not answer.*) You there. I said, what's your name?

ELLEN-A-DALE

Ellen.

SHERIFF

Well, Ellen, why don't you . . . dance for me. (*She begins to dance again. Robin of Locksley appears on a mound overlooking the scene. He is young and dressed in white. As he moves down through the crowd, Ellen-a-Dale stops dancing. The crowd becomes quiet and everyone turns to look at Robin. Silence. There is a burst of high, thin laughter from Maureen. Silence.*)

ROBIN

(*to Ellen-a-Dale*) Hello. (*Maureen laughs again. Someone slaps her, and she says "Oooh!" Silence. Robin speaks to Ellen-a-Dale again.*) That was a lovely dance. Why did you stop? (*The Sheriff's men mimic him: "Oh, why did you stop, why did you stop?" Robin speaks to Ellen-a-Dale again.*) You're going to Nottingham Fair? (*Alan-a-Dale, who has been playing the drum, speaks for Ellen-a-Dale.*)

ALAN-A-DALE

Yes.

ROBIN

Me, too. (*The Sheriff's men mock him: "Me, too! Me, too!" "A lovely dance!" "Me, too!" Robin turns toward them. Silence.*)

SHERIFF

Hello. What's your name?

ROBIN

Robin. What's yours? (*Voices: "What?" "What's his name?" "Rude dog!" "Doesn't know his place." "That's the Sheriff you're talking to, boy!"*)

SHERIFF

So *nice* to meet you, Robin. My name is John. The Sheriff of Nottingham. Tell me, Robin, what are you going to do at the fair?

ROBIN

I'm going to win the prize for my lady. (*This is greeted with laughter and more comments: "Oh, he's going to win the prize for his lady." "Who's his lady?" "His mother's milk is still wet on his lips." "Watch now, he'll be mixing ale with his milk soon."*)

SHERIFF

Very good, Robin. And how are you going to win the prize?

ROBIN

> With my bow, sir. (*More laughter: "There's a twopenny bow for you!" "The boy's as green as his wood."*) I happen to be a very good shot.

SHERIFF

> No-o-o! Prove it.

ROBIN

> There's a herd of deer, yonder in the wood. See it?

SHERIFF

> Yes . . . I see it.

ROBIN

> I'll drop one of them deer for you. (*The men and the Sheriff exchange glances.*)

SHERIFF

> Yes. Yes, Robin, I'd like to see that very much . . . very, very much.

ROBIN

> Give me room, then. (*The onlookers arrange themselves. Robin takes aim.*)

SHERIFF

> Wait!

ROBIN

> What?

SHERIFF

> This is too easy. There's plenty deer in that herd. With a little luck any boy could shoot in their midst and bring one down. Which deer will it be, Robin?

ROBIN

> Pick one, then, why don't you.

SHERIFF

> I want the white buck, by the oak. (*Robin takes aim again and shoots. A woman's short cry is the sound of the dying buck. There is silence for a moment, then a long "oooooh" from the crowd.*) Very well done, Robin. You've a fine eye and a strong arm. It's such a shame, though. You see, you've just killed one of the King's deer. (*The onlookers gasp and exclaim: "The King's*

deer!'' ''He's killed one of the King's deer!'') You killed one of
the King's deer, Robin. That's a crime, Robin. I place two
hundred gold coins on this man's head. Dead or alive.

ROBIN

But you said . . . I don't understand . . . You all wanted me
to . . . (*Robin breaks through the menacing throng of the
Sheriff's men. They approach him, stalking him as a cat stalks a
mouse: "That's a crime!" "One of the King's deer!" "Two
hundred gold coins!" "Dead or alive!" "They'll cut off your ears
and brand you for a poacher!" "That's a crime!" Robin takes an
arrow from his quiver and fits it to his bow.*) Stand back, now. Let
me pass. (*The crowd makes way for him as he moves slowly
toward the mound. The Sheriff signals one of his men. The man
draws an arrow and takes aim at Robin. Ellen-a-Dale screams
"Robin!" and pushes the bowman's arm upward. Robin wheels,
draws an arrow, and lets it fly. The young man screams, turns with
an arrow in his chest, falls, and dies. Robin runs down to him.
Voices in the crowd gasp: "He's killed him!" "He's murdered
him!"*)

SHERIFF

Get him! Kill him! (*His words are echoed by his men. Robin
rushes upstage, climbing over the men's backs. Shouting, drums,
and "chase" music fill the air. A series of light shifts and rapid
blackouts allow glimpses of Robin and the Sheriff's men thrashing
about in the wood and fighting. The lights come up on Robin,
alone and exhausted. He drops to his knees and collapses. The
lights fade.*)

Scene i   Dawn in the Deep Wood

It is very early on a summer morning. The stillness of the gray dawn is broken by a solitary birdcall. One by one, other birds join in a joyous crescendo culminating in a rooster's crow. The rooster's crow is followed immediately by a loud splash, and the gray light is pierced with red. Suddenly a head pops up. Robin's bare back is seen in the same spot where he collapsed. Bewildered, he looks around with a long, loud laugh. He stretches and shakes himself, then falls to his knees and splashes water from the brook onto his face. Rising, he pulls a green mantle over his shoulders and moves slowly offstage, following the brook. A baby cries. Soft mother-talk is heard. The focus shifts to Ellen-a-Dale with her child.

ELLEN-A-DALE

Hush! Hush, now. Hushabye, darling, down to your toes. Alan. Alan, wake up, it's morning.

ALAN-A-DALE

(*yawning*) What? Ohhhh! (*He kisses Ellen-a-Dale and speaks to the baby.*) You, now, shush up. Shoosh! Little Prince Shooshabina. What you want is a good smack. (*He kisses the baby.*) There. Watch me now, or I'll do it again.

ELLEN-A-DALE

He's hungry.

ALAN-A-DALE

So am I, lady, so am I.

ELLEN-A-DALE

I think I'll take him away from the sleepers. (*Members of the sleeping band begin to move and mumble, awakening. As Ellen-*

a-Dale passes upstage, she stumbles against a mound of green. The mound, Friar Tuck, barks like a dog, sits up, and looks around; the barking falters and Tuck groans. Ellen laughs.) Oh! Tuck!

TUCK

Good morning, Ellen. (*Tuck settles back to sleep. Ellen-a-Dale leaves. A young boy, crouching in the overhanging branches of a tree, immediately begins to bark like a dog.*) What! A dog in the tree? Alan, there is a dog in the tree! (*Much jumps from the tree onto Tuck's stomach, laughing and barking.*) Oh! Twenty Hail Marys before breakfast . . . Oof! Sixty! And two hundred Our Fathers. A novena! Oh, you wretch. Get off. On your knees, boy! (*Tuck sits up, grabs a stick, and smacks the boy. Much shrieks and runs away with Tuck following him; Tuck trips and falls. Just then Robin appears.*)

MUCH

Robin, catch! (*Much makes a flying leap onto Robin's shoulders.*)

ROBIN

It's Much the Miller's son! So you're still here, are you?

MUCH

Of course I am, Robin. Where else would I be?

ROBIN

Oh, you never know where you might be when you wake up in the morning. I never do.

TUCK

That little wretch jumped on my stomach!

ROBIN

Tuck, you old fatty! Good day to you!

TUCK

Bread and water for a fortnight. He'll be whipped.

ROBIN

I'll take care of it. (*Robin grabs Much around the middle and swings him around until they both fall down.*) Much, go get some wood for the fire.

MUCH

I don't know where it is, Robin.

ROBIN

> (*mimicking Much*) I don't know where it is, Robin! (*Robin gives Much a playful kick in the pants to set him off and crosses to a family grouped around a small campfire.*) Good morning, Eleanor. How did you pass the night?

ELEANOR

> Fine, and you, Robin? (*Alan-a-Dale begins to sing to himself.*)

ALAN-A-DALE

> *When the sun is a-dawning*
> *And water I'm drawing*
> *I think of the Lady of Dale.*
>
> *I drop down a bucket*
> *And if I'm in luck it*
> *Will bring up the Lady of Dale.*

ROBIN

> Lovely, Alan, I hear you. Sing us a bit now, will you? (*Ellen-a-Dale enters, carrying the baby. She stops behind Robin and listens.*) Let's have another verse, Alan. (*Several members of the group join Alan-a-Dale in the song.*)

ALAN-A-DALE

> *When the sun in the summer*
> *Is beating and burning*
> *I toss down a bucket of ale.*
>
> *I toss down a bucket*
> *And hope I come up with*
> *Another big bucket of ale.*
>
> *The summer sun's setting*
> *And my thoughts are turning*
> *Right back to that Lady of Dale.*
>
> *Tossing and turning*
> *And in my bed yearning*
> *And all for that Lady of Dale.*

(*The song fades away as the members of the group begin their morning work.*)

ELLEN-A-DALE

Good morning, Robin.

ROBIN

Good morning, Ellen. That boy of yours has a tongue in his head, don't he? He looks like his mother. (*Ellen-a-Dale curtsies and goes to sit beside Alan-a-Dale. Robin crosses to where Scarlet is sleeping and speaks to him.*) Scarlet! Scarlet, wake up now!

SCARLET

I'm awake.

ROBIN

I want you to do me a favor, Scarlet.

SCARLET

What is it?

ROBIN

Try looking pretty today. Anyways, do your best, man.

SCARLET

(*laughing*) I'll see you at noon, Robin! (*Robin begins to rouse the other sleepers. Shirtless men enter and cross to the stream to wash, grunting and muttering morning greetings. Hairy chests are scratched and then covered. A number of conversations are going on simultaneously: "Hello, Harry. You're looking awful." "First it was the birds, and then it was the baby." "Morning, Robin!" "Get a fire going, will you?" All eventually join in singing "The Lady of Dale." Some of them dance.*)

ROBIN

(*picking up a large stone and addressing it in a big voice*) Stone! (*He kisses it.*) Stone, go ask a fish the time of day, will you please? (*There is laughter from the band as he tosses the stone toward the brook. The stone hits Tuck, who is washing.*)

TUCK

Ouch! Who threw that stone? It hit me on the head! (*Robin grabs a tambourine from a little girl and puts it on his head. He speaks in a falsetto voice.*)

ROBIN

> I must own to my actions. It was I, Friar Tuck, your own true love.

TUCK

> Well, you're a goose, Robin Hood, I've always said
> so . . . Peterkin! Lift me up. (*Peterkin reaches out to help
> Tuck.*)

ROBIN

> Peterkin! Let him down. (*Peterkin lets go of Tuck, who sits down
> again quickly. All laugh.*) I know all about it, Tuck. You don't
> have to tell me. I agree. This boy here (*indicating Much*) is the
> silliest goose I've ever known. But just sit down again, Tuck,
> make yourself comfortable, and listen while I tell you. I had a
> dream. (*There is applause and genuine interest from the band.*)
> Yes, I did. I lay in the long grass by the river's edge, and I dreamt I
> held a woman by the green of her hair. I dreamt I held my Marion
> by her long green hair.

MUCH

> What? Marion's hair isn't green.

ROBIN

> (*letting Much drop from his shoulders*) Jump! Splash! River-
> daughter was gone, and I woke up with two fistfuls of grass. (*All
> laugh.*)

MUCH

> (*crawling around behind Robin while Tuck pokes at him with his
> stick*) Marion's hair is brown, like chestnuts are brown.

ROBIN

> No, that's one thing you just can't be sure of.

MUCH

> What is?

ROBIN

> Where you might be when you wake up in the morning. It's been
> an awful problem for me, let me tell you. One fine morning, I
> woke up in . . . (*thinking*) a hurry. Yes I did.

TUCK

> Simple. One of the Sheriff's dogs got hold of your pants.

ELLEN-A-DALE

The Friar woke up this morning and thought he WAS one of the Sheriff's dogs.

ROBIN

Dawn of another day, I opened my eyes and I was in love. Picture that. The breeze was blowing and the grass was growing and I was in love. I was so scared, I didn't move till noon. (*Laughter. Ellis shouts from the bridge, holding a trout.*)

ELLIS

Caught one, Robin!

ROBIN

Good. Catch a dozen more and we'll have breakfast! (*Conversations take place in the background among the members of the band.*)

TUCK

Don't forget the evil mornings, Robin. Days when the sun was ashamed to shine on the land. A body didn't know where he was then, did he?

HOB

No, he din't and that's a fack.

ALAN-A-DALE

Lion-hearted Richard gone from England. His black-hearted brother putting the fear of darkness into good men's souls.

SCARLET

Fear of the night. The night. Fear of the holy night. (*Several voices are raised in agreement, each trying to tell his own story.*)

DERRY

He took my lands and killed my dogs!

HOB

Me old mother, she . . .

JON

I shot a deer so I could feed my family . . .

HARRY

We were hungry and it was cold.

TOM

It was the Abbot took my lands.

JULIAN

The Sheriff said he would cut off my ears if he caught me. Well, he isn't going to catch me!

FRANK

And it was so cold . . .

HOB

Me old mother, she took a broom to the Sheriff hisself, she did. But then the Sheriff took me mother for a old broom and swept up good. Mad? Oh, she was mad as bees . . .

BOB

Bees? I used to raise bees, once. (*A small groan comes from the men, who know how Bob runs on.*) Me and my wife did, God warm her soul in heaven. Nine little hives that stood in the shade of a big copper beech. Made a circle right 'round the trunk. Swollen fat, and dripping honey out the sides like gold was running in the sun. We didn't have no children, see . . .

MUCH

What's for breakfast?

TUCK

Oatmeal and trout for the gentlemen. For you, a nasty yellow fish.

MUCH

Oatmeal with honey on?

BOB

Those little hives was a great pleasure to me and my wife. Humming and whining the day long. My wife's name was Margaret.

ALAN-A-DALE

Today's the day, ain't it, Robin? Your wife's coming back to us?

ROBIN

THERE is music, Alan-a-Dale. Marion's on her way. I feel her near, like she was looking at me with all her eyes.

BOB

Well, anyways, King Richard went off south to find him the Holy

Land, may the Blessed Virgin bring him back quick, and all the troubles began. Which you all know as well as I do. Well, anyways, one day we hear a noise out back, sounds like all the Turks in Turkey out to get them a Christian man. It was the bees kicking up a fuss. I looked up at Margaret and I said, "What's got into the bees?" Well, she didn't know. So I went out beneath the copper beech myself, and there was one of the Sheriff's new men, ugly as a cart horse, poking at the hives as bold as y' please. Well, I asked him his business. He turned to me with his horse's face and he said, "Those is the King's bees, man, and you will turn them over to the Sheriff." Well, I looked him back and I said, "These bees is the Lord's bees, sir, you will take your horse's face straight away. Won't you." Well, when my wife hears that, she just had to laugh, and that didn't set well with Horse-Face either. To make a long story short — maybe it ain't short enough, I don't know — in short, then, I lost my house and I lost my lands. To the Sheriff. I lost my bees. Margaret, she passed on soon after. And where I was when I woke up was here. In short. (*There is a silence among the group which indicates their sympathy for Bob's story. Bob is embarrassed but wishes he could think of a little more.*)

ROBIN

(*quietly*) Bob Smith. Yes. The morning came for each one of us here when he found himself — or herself, begging your pardon, ladies — smack outside the law. Outlaw. Out of law. Out of town, out of home and farm, out of family, and out, into the wood. (*pause*) But such talk for a day like today. Besides, the King is coming. Coming back soon, I feel it. Do you believe me?

BOB

I don't know but what they cut down the copper beech, too. Now that would be a shame. (*Alan-a-Dale has been strumming throughout Bob's speech, and now he begins to sing "The Golden Pear."* * *He is joined gradually by several others.*)

ALAN-A-DALE

(*singing*)

*Music on page 195.

Through green and gold and green again,
The dawn and the midday, the nightfall and dream,
Through summer and autumn, through winter and spring,
We keep the wood and we seek our own king.

The king is coming, we light the pyre.
The bloom of summer's love feeds the fire,
The blood of autumn is gilding the flame
And winter's chill is fled for shame.

For shame is none of our lot cast.
We seek the dawn and recall the past.
The heart of lion, brave Richard's reign —
Our lion-hearted, he's coming again.

HUGH

(*after a pause*) I'm hungry.

ROBIN

Breakfast?

TUCK

Oatmeal and trout.

ROBIN

Breakfast! (*The members of the band begin to gather in groups and to leave the stage.*) Much! (*pulling Much back by his shirttail*) Answer me this one. You heard the cuckoo-birds singing their heads off this morning. Now tell me, where are you when you can't hear the cuckoo? Where might you be when you wake up and the cuckoo's cry stops short? (*snapping his fingers*) Like that? Give up?

MUCH

No.

ROBIN

Tuck knows. Climb on his back while he takes you to breakfast, and he'll tell you. (*Much climbs on Tuck's back; they waddle off.*)

TUCK

You'd be in autumn, boy. Autumn. Summer'd be over and done

with. Gone. Autumn. (*They exit. Only Scarlet and Robin are left onstage.*)

SCARLET

(*as if he were calling after Much*) And after autumn comes winter, right, Much? And then do you know where you are, when there's cold winds and winter? Do you? You're right here, that's where you are.

ROBIN

Scarlet.

SCARLET

(*to Robin*) You're right here.

ROBIN

(*speaking to a stone he holds in his hand*) You know, Scarlet's only problem is his hair. Redheads have an awful time of it.

SCARLET

(*playfully but with menace*) Robin. Robin, what are you doing? (*quietly*) Oh, nothing. (*suddenly animated*) Look, Robin. I can do it, too.

ROBIN

What's that, Scarlet?

SCARLET

Magic, Robin. Watch now. See that tree?

ROBIN

(*wearily, used to this*) Yes.

SCARLET

Do you see it? Are you watching it? Magic, Robin. A magic trick. Are you watching that tree? Good. (*pointing at the tree and speaking to it*) Tree! Don't move! (*Pause. Then Scarlet begins to laugh. Robin also laughs. Suddenly Scarlet grips Robin's arm in a wrestling hold.*) Magic, Robin. I can do it, too. (*He spars with Robin.*)

ROBIN

I thought so. (*He catches Scarlet's legs and trips him.*) I thought so. (*They wrestle continuously throughout the following dialogue.*) Listen. Scarlet. You know what I'm going to do?

SCARLET

(*becoming more intent on the wrestling*) No. No, I don't, Robin.

ROBIN

Well, I'm going to set up some little beehives. Do you believe me?

SCARLET

No. Yes. I don't care what you do, Robin.

ROBIN

Nine little beehives, all in a circle round that tree there. Wait until old Bob sees that.

SCARLET

(*still wrestling and sparring*) Fine, Robin. That will be fine.

ROBIN

I knew you'd think so. Oh, it'll be very fine, indeed. Bob will be the beekeeper, all his own. In charge of . . . all the bees. You see, Scarlet, we just have to wait. And work. That's all. Everything will come. Everything's on its way.

SCARLET

Doesn't it ever *bother* you, Robin?

ROBIN

What?

SCARLET

Did you ever find out what his name was?

ROBIN

Whose name?

SCARLET

(*throwing Robin to the ground*) The man you killed!

ROBIN

(*from the ground*) Scarlet. Don't. Please. Just don't. Don't do it.

SCARLET

Don't you tell me anything!

ROBIN

(*getting up*) Don't you see, everything's on its way already. Marion's coming. The King will come. You believe me, don't you? Don't you believe me? (*He throws Scarlet to the ground. Scarlet lies still.*) Believe me, Scarlet? Scarlet? (*kneeling beside Scarlet*) Scarlet! Most Holy and Blessed Virgin, save him! (*Scarlet opens his eyes, looks around, and then quickly boxes Robin's ears. They both laugh, relieved.*) How are you, man?

SCARLET

How am I? I want a drink, that's how I am. Give me a drink, someone. (*He affects a Scottish accent.*) For I've a wee pain in me head.

ROBIN

(*still standing over Scarlet and laughing*) It's not even noon yet. I'll make you breakfast.

SCARLET

I don't want breakfast. I want to get drunk. (*Pause. Scarlet looks up at Robin.*) You're a real fool, you know that, Robin?

ROBIN

Yes, I know. I know what you mean. (*Robin turns and walks away slowly. The lights fade on Scarlet.*)

SCARLET

A real fool. (*Blackout.*)

Scene ii   A Storm

Thunder and lightning. Horses' hooves and neighing are heard. As the orchestra begins to play "The Sheriff's Song," men emerge from the darkness of the storm. They wear black capes and hangman's hoods. The Sheriff and the Abbot ride among them. The men trudge in mud downstage, pushing a peasant man before them. Two men shove him to the ground and hold him.*

SHERIFF

(*to the peasant*) Where did you get it, if you didn't shoot it?

PEASANT

What do you mean?

*Music on page 195.

SHERIFF

Teach him courtesy, boys. (*Two men push the peasant's face into the mud.*) The deer, man. Where did you get that deer?

PEASANT

It was a gift.

ABBOT

A gift! How very nice! (*The Sheriff's men ad-lib comments: "Oh, it was a gift!" "A birthday present?" "Someone shot a deer and gave it to him!" "How nice for you!"*)

SHERIFF

Maybe you and Prince John are good friends. Does he give you presents very often? Maybe he sends you a lot of his deer. Teach him not to lie, boys. (*They kick him.*)

PEASANT

It's not a lie. He gave it to me.

SHERIFF

Who did? Prince John?

PEASANT

(*wailing*) No.

SHERIFF

Then who was it? Who gave you one of the King's deer? (*Silence. One of the Sheriff's men grips the peasant by the hair.*) Was it . . . a man named Robin?

PEASANT

(*after a pause*) Yes. Yes, it was a man named Robin of Hood.

SHERIFF

(*laughs*) A man named Robin of Hood! I thought so. You see, years ago a man named Robin shot one of the King's deer, and he's been shooting them ever since. Answer me, now, if you want to keep your ears. Where is he? (*Scarlet enters, drunk, from the wood.*)

SCARLET

Where is he? I'm right here!

SHERIFF

Who is that?

SCARLET

What? My name is Scarlet — Will Scarlet — and I'll knock the man down who says I'm not.

SHERIFF

But where is Robin Hood?

SCARLET

I couldn't tell you. But I know who he is. He's a fool, that's who he is.

ABBOT

(*indicating Scarlet*) Who is that?

SCARLET

Dammit, Father, I just told you. He's a fool, and he knows it, too.

SHERIFF

No, who are you?

SCARLET

My God. Who are these people? I said, my name is Scarlet, Will Scarlet.

SHERIFF

Do you know a man called Robin Hood?

SCARLET

No. I don't know him. I don't know the man. (*to the peasant lying in the mud*) Who are you, a fairy princess? Come dance with me. Oh. No. This lady's got mud on her face!

SHERIFF

The man is mad. We're wasting our time. Move on! (*They trudge off, pushing the peasant before them. Scarlet sits down in a puddle, pulls out a jug, and drinks.*)

SCARLET

(*calling after the Sheriff and his men*) Maybe the next dance! (*He drinks.*) I don't know him. The man's mad. (*Blackout.*)

Scene iii   The Archery Contest

The lights come up immediately on Robin and a half dozen of his archers. They stand together with bows, looking off into the clearing.

ROBIN

> (*shouting offstage*) Are you ready, Friar Tuck? (*silence*) I think he fell asleep! (*laughter*) Tuck, are you ready? (*Tuck's shout, from a great distance, is heard only faintly.*)

TUCK

> Fire at will! (*Instantly several dozen volleys of arrows fly off into the clearing — fft! fft! fft! fft! The men respond with ad-libs and laughter.*)

ROBIN

> Don't hit the judge, boys! You're aiming for the target, not Friar Tuck. Did you see him jump? (*The men laugh.*) Tuck! How are you, man?

TUCK

> (*shouting, virtually incoherent*) Watch out, you fools! (*The men laugh and draw another round of arrows. They fire and ad-lib: "Mine's on!" "Too high." "Where did it go?" "There's a wind."*)

ROBIN

> Friar Tuck! How do they lie?

TUCK

> (*unintelligibly*) Coshee yooshell!

ROBIN

> What?

TUCK

> Come and see for yourself!

ROBIN

> You're the judge, man! Are you going to make me walk a hundred fifty yards?

TUCK

> Yes!

ROBIN

> What? Oh, never mind. I'll run down and see who wins for today. Help Much there with his bow while I'm gone, will you? (*Robin runs off. The archers gather around Much.*)

ELLIS

> I don't know how we're going to help him with his bow. Do you think you can lift it, boy?

MUCH

> Of course I can lift it.

FRANK

> I'm not sure. It's pretty heavy, you know. But if you think you can lift it, why don't you try to string it? (*Frank unstrings one of the bows and hands it to Much.*)

ELLIS

> Come on, Much, bend that bow.

HOB

> He can't do it!

FRANK

> Give it here.

MUCH

> I can do it. Give me a chance. I've done it a hundred times. (*The men laugh.*)

ELLIS

> A hundred times!

BOB

> (*taking the bow gently from Much and stringing it*) No, it's true. I seen him do it six hundred times. (*They laugh.*) Now, give him a chance, give him room.

FRANK

> There's your bow. Now pull that string back to your ear! (*Much struggles unsuccessfully with the bow.*)

ELLIS

Maybe you should pull with both your hands! (*Laughter. Robin enters with Friar Tuck on his shoulders.*)

TUCK

Off to see the Pope!

ROBIN

Attention! Attention! The judge has arrived. Prizes! (*The men ad-lib: "Prizes!" "Who won?" "Mine was on, I know it was."*)

TUCK

Silence, my dear sirs. I must beg you to be quiet, while I tell you. The winner of the . . . third prize is . . . Ellis Baker! A piping hot kidney pie for you, Ellis, we're proud of you. (*The men cheer.*)

ROBIN

(*to Tuck, still on his shoulders*) Really, Tuck, this is too much to bear.

TUCK

The second place goes to . . . young Ron Tice! The prize for second place . . . a fine leather belt! (*The men cheer.*)

ROBIN

I know you're all waiting to hear who the first place winner is. (*He groans.*) I can't wait myself.

TUCK

The first prize for the day, for excellence of aim and strength of arm, goes to Robin Hood! (*The men cheer.*) And for his prize, he . . .

ROBIN

He gets to carry the judge! (*The men cheer.*)

TUCK

Gentlemen! Off you go! Fine work, all of you. And, Robin, for his prize, must walk sixty paces as penance, with a man of God on his back! (*The archers depart singing "The Lady of Dale." Robin, Tuck, and Much remain onstage. Robin paces with Tuck on his back. While Robin paces, Much is trying to pull the string on his bow back to his ear.*)

MUCH

Robin! How am I doing?

ROBIN

You've got to get the string back to your cheek, Much. All the way back, so you could stick your thumb in your ear. If you wanted to. Tuck, really. (*to Much*) Which you probably wouldn't, but you know what I mean.

TUCK

Off to see the Pope! (*During the next speech Robin sinks first to his knees, then sprawls flat on the ground with Tuck sitting on his shoulders.*)

ROBIN

When you get it back that far, back to your ear, you can send an arrow halfway to town and back.

TUCK

(*stepping off Robin's shoulders, lifting his robe daintily*) Thank you. Much, we're going. Good-bye.

MUCH

It wasn't that bad, was it, Robin?

ROBIN

(*misunderstanding him*) Unbearable. I'll never walk again. (*Much laughs.*) Oh. No. Not bad at all, but you've got to get it back to your ear. (*Tuck and Much exit.*)

Scene iv   Little John and
the Passing of Summer

Robin stands, humming; he picks up the bow and the quiver that Much left lying on the ground and slings them over his shoulder. He sits down on the end of the log bridge over the stream, takes an apple from a pouch, and begins to eat it. Little John, an immense man, enters and stands on the opposite end of the log.

LITTLE JOHN

　　Get off the bridge!

ROBIN

　　(*startled*) What?

LITTLE JOHN

　　Get off the bridge!

ROBIN

　　(*laughing*) And why should I do that, sir?

LITTLE JOHN

　　(*sneezing*) Aaachoo! Because I'm coming over.

ROBIN

　　Well, bless you! And when I've crossed the bridge, and am on my way, you may certainly cross over.

LITTLE JOHN

　　I'm coming over now. You see, I've been taking a little nap, and now I'm ready to move on. So you'll have to get off the bridge. (*Brief pause. Robin tosses his apple core into the brook.*) Tell me, little man, who shot that arrow?

ROBIN

　　What arrow?

LITTLE JOHN

(*holding up a single arrow*) *This* arrow. I took a nap beneath that tree, there, and when I woke up, there was this arrow sitting on my head. Or it might be I woke up when the arrow sat there. Who shot it?

ROBIN

Who wants to know?

LITTLE JOHN

(*wearily*) Oh, my. (*straightening up to his full height*) John Little wants to know.

ROBIN

Oh. Well. It was a little boy, Mister . . .

LITTLE JOHN

Little.

ROBIN

That's right, about twelve years old. You'll find him half a mile down Watling Road. You'd know him if you saw him. Now, if you'll excuse me, I'll be on my way.

LITTLE JOHN

(*making one stride and blocking the way across the bridge*) Aaachoo!

ROBIN

Bless you.

LITTLE JOHN

Thank you.

ROBIN

You've caught a cold.

LITTLE JOHN

Ah! A cold. Yes, I've caught a cold.

ROBIN

You're a bigger man, aren't you? Than most.

LITTLE JOHN

My mother thought so. (*Robin laughs.*) Of course, she was a bigger woman.

ROBIN and LITTLE JOHN

> (*not quite simultaneously*) Than most.

LITTLE JOHN

> Yes. (*laughing*) Say, you're not going to get off this bridge, are you?

ROBIN

> (*laughing*) No. I'm not. I don't suppose you . . . .

LITTLE JOHN

> (*laughing harder*) Not a chance.

ROBIN

> It's not a very big bridge.

LITTLE JOHN

> It's a small bridge.

ROBIN

> Teeny-tiny little bridge.

LITTLE JOHN

> Tiniest little bridge I ever saw in my life. (*He immediately stops laughing.*) What was that you were saying about my mother?

ROBIN

> What? Here, now, one of us will just have to get off. The bridge is very narrow, you see.

LITTLE JOHN

> One way or another.

ROBIN

> What? (*With one movement he draws an arrow from his quiver and notches it to his bow.*) I could always put an arrow through you and be on my way.

LITTLE JOHN

> Aaachoo! You could, you could. But then you'd be quite the coward, wouldn't you, since I have nothing in my hands but a little bit of wood. (*He plants an enormous staff squarely in front of him. Robin draws back the string of his bow, then shoots down into the water.*)

ROBIN

> Trout. The brook is full of them. Taste nice later on, don't you think? Well, I'm no coward, Mister . . .

LITTLE JOHN
> Little!

ROBIN
> That's right. So I'd better cut me a staff like yours. You'll wait right here, won't you? You wouldn't come straight over the bridge while I'm . . .

LITTLE JOHN
> Say, what do you take me for?

ROBIN
> Forgive me. I don't know what came over me. (*He steps off the bridge, lays down his bow and quiver, takes out a knife, and hacks off a branch of a nearby tree.*) I won't be a moment. (*Robin inspects his new staff, looks at Little John — who sneezes — and then back at the staff, and throws it away. He cuts off a gigantic branch and whittles off the twigs. Then he steps onto the bridge and takes a deep breath. Little John steps forward, swinging his staff above his head, and they begin to fight. The battle is punctuated by sneezes and occasional periods of rest in which the two men lean on their staffs and pant. During a lull Robin speaks.*) What brings you to Sherwood?

LITTLE JOHN
> Looking for someone.

ROBIN
> Lovely hereabouts, don't you think? (*Little John lunges at Robin, and they begin again. Little John stops to sneeze. He pulls out a huge red handkerchief to blow his nose, bending over with the force of the sneeze. Robin whacks his backside with his staff.*)

LITTLE JOHN
> (*in a rage*) Oooooh! (*They fight again, and then there is another lull.*)

ROBIN
> Who is it you're looking for?

LITTLE JOHN
> Man named Robin. Robin of Hood.

ROBIN
> What do you want with this Robin Hood fellow?

LITTLE JOHN

I'm bleeding. Oh. You'll pay, little man. (*They fight again. Then Robin suddenly stops and points behind Little John.*)

ROBIN

Say, your mother IS a bigger woman than most!

LITTLE JOHN

What?

ROBIN

Your mother, man!

LITTLE JOHN

(*turning and looking in the direction in which Robin is pointing*) Mother? (*Robin whacks him on his backside again. The fight resumes. The blows continue during the next exchange.*)

ROBIN

Really, now, why do you want to find this Robin Hood?

LITTLE JOHN

I've got a message for him. From his lady, Marion.

ROBIN

(*stopping still*) What?

LITTLE JOHN

Aaachoo! (*He knocks Robin off the bridge into the brook and laughs. Robin flounders, then sits up and laughs himself.*) Where are you now, little fellow?

ROBIN

In the river, you big brute. (*lying back*) I think I'll just float out to sea. (*Robin sees the arrow that he shot earlier sticking into the river bed. He pulls it out and there is a trout on the end of it. He offers the trout to Little John.*) Have it. It's yours. You won it. (*Little John takes one end of the arrow, whereupon Robin pulls him into the brook.*) You want to be careful. You'll catch your death of cold.

LITTLE JOHN

Aaachoo! (*Bob enters carrying his bow and quiver and a catch of rabbits.*)

BOB

Hello, Robin. What are you doing?

ROBIN

I'm bathing with an old friend who would like to join our band. What do you say to that?

BOB

Well, is he nice?

ROBIN

(*to Little John*) Well, are you nice?

LITTLE JOHN

(*blowing his nose*) Very nice.

BOB

Then it's all right with me, Robin. He'll have to have a name, though. What are we going to call him?

LITTLE JOHN

(*to Robin*) Robin? Robin of Hood?

BOB

No, that's his name. (*indicating Robin*)

ROBIN

(*to Little John*) Pleased to meet you. (*They wrestle in recognition, laughing. Alan-a-Dale, Tuck, Much, Peterkin, and others enter with jugs of ale, rabbits, and strings of fish.*)

ALAN-A-DALE

(*to Bob*) What's he doing down there?

BOB

It's Robin having a bath with a man who's very nice.

ROBIN

Won't you join me? (*All laugh.*)

BOB

But we don't know what to call him.

ALAN-A-DALE

Well, ask him his name if you don't know what to call him.

BOB

A good idea! (*laughter*)

ROBIN

Then you've seen Marion today, have you?

LITTLE JOHN

Yes, and she's a lovely lady. Aaachoo! (*Little John stands up and all gasp and murmur when they see how large he is.*)

BOB

What's your name? (*quickly, in a stage whisper*) What's his name?

ROBIN

His name is John . . . Little. (*laughter*) But that won't do, will it? What'll it be?

BOB

How about Little John? (*All laugh and shout in agreement.*)

TUCK

A christening! Bring the baby to me. Bring the child unto me! (*The men of the band surround and lift Little John in an action like that of the Lilliputians overpowering Gulliver. They hold him aloft, spread-eagled and facing the ground with his head toward the audience.*) Who bringeth this babe to be christened?

ROBIN

That do I. (*Little John struggles.*)

TUCK

And what name nameth you him?

ROBIN

Him name I Little John.

TUCK

That'll do. Welcome to our band, Little John. (*He empties a jug of ale over Little John's head. All laugh, and there is a general uproar. Little John breaks away from his captors. Tuck is trapped. Others are behind Little John, who is at the center.*)

LITTLE JOHN

(*grabbing his staff*) Oh, I'll give you welcome on your backside, Father, you just watch! (*Amid shrieks and laughter from the men Friar Tuck lifts up his skirts and runs as Little John, wet and sneezing, pursues him. Robin and the rest follow them out, leaving Much alone onstage. Much sees Robin's bow and quiver by the bridge. He looks about him to see that he is alone. Then he takes the bow, notches an arrow, and draws the string back. He takes aim at a circling hawk in the direction of the balcony. Then he stops following the bird with the bow, eases the string back, drops the arrow to the ground, and unstrings the bow. He shakes his head.)*

MUCH

I can't get it back. Just can't get it back to my ear, that's all. Well, go on then, you old hawk! Laughing at me, ain't you. Go on back to your nest and laugh. Tell all your little hawk-babies about Much the Miller's son who can't pull the string back to his ear. (*He pauses and looks at the bow.*) But I'll bet I can balance this thing on my hand. (*Much "tightropes" across the log bridge, balancing Robin's bow on his hand. Bob enters, carrying Ellen-a-Dale's baby as if it were made of eggshells.*)

BOB

They gave me the baby, but I don't know what to do with him. Everybody's in a state. Shoutings and goings on, and I don't know what else. Why can't folks just sit down somewhere? Too much for him and me both, wasn't it?

MUCH

I had a hawk in my sights. Great big one. Biggest hawk I ever saw.

BOB

What am I going to do with this baby? Round face, red as a cherry . . . Looks like he's about to explode.

MUCH

I let him go, though. Let him fly off home to his family. Gosh, he was big.

BOB

Too much noise for the both of us. The new man, that big fellow, he brought a message from Marion. Met her in the wood. Said she'd be home by late afternoon, but some Sheriff's man seen her, and she had to be careful.

MUCH

(*running to Bob*) Marion's coming? Today? Oh, Bob!

BOB

Mind the baby! Easy, Much.

MUCH

You know, Bob, sometimes I wish I were grown up, like Robin. And sometimes I want to be as small as that baby there.

BOB

Of course, when Robin heard about Marion, he started hopping around like a madman. I told him, I said, if anyone can take care of herself, it's Marion. I don't think he heard me, though. You want to be little again?

MUCH

No.

BOB

Well, you can't be. You know, this morning it felt like summer would last forever, and now it's like it's all over. Will you tell me what I'm supposed to do with this child?

MUCH

Sing to him.

BOB

(*nervously*) What? I don't know how to sing to a baby. (*Bob sits down with the child on his lap; Much stands behind him with his arms leaning on Bob's shoulders. Much dangles a blossom above the baby's face.*)

MUCH

Sing to him. Come on, I'll help you. (*The first measures of "Horses Are Running"* * are heard.*)

MUCH and BOB

(*singing*)

> Horses are running,
> Sleep my little baby.
> Fishes are laughing
> When the twilight falls.
>
> Where is the child?

*Music on page 196.

Where's the little baby?
Lying asleep,
In his own cradle.

BOB

Much, look at him smile! Did you ever see a little baby smile like that? (*They begin to sing again.*)

ELLEN-A-DALE

(*calling from offstage*) Bob Smith! Bob?

BOB

(*breaking off his song*) What? Oh. Here, Ellen!

ELLEN-A-DALE

(*entering*) Thank you, Bob. (*She starts to take the child.*) Was he a lot of trouble?

BOB

Oh, well. You know, I know how to handle babies. (*Again Ellen-a-Dale moves to take the baby.*) No, no, that's all right, Ellen. I'll carry him. I'll just carry him for you. No, no trouble at all. We sang and we laughed . . . (*Bob, Ellen-a-Dale, and the baby exit, talking.*)

MUCH

(*softly, to himself*) Good-bye, baby. (*He watches them leave. The colored lights have begun to change from green to gold. Birds singing in the background suddenly fall silent. Much looks about him. He picks up the bow and lies down on his back. He holds the bow above him and tries to pull the string to his ear as the lights fade.*)

Scene v   Autumn in the Clearing

During the last moments of the preceding scene the forest undergoes many changes. The green lights of summer on the leaves and the boughs first intensify, then become moving shafts of gold and red. These changes take place almost imperceptibly. The spread tail of a peacock is caught briefly in a shaft of light and then disappears. The bell of a country church is heard far away. Members of the band are gathered onstage, sitting on the ground, sorting grains and fruits of the harvest. They call to one another, laugh, and talk together. A shaft of light reveals Much still lying on the ground with the bow above his head. A voice calls from offstage to announce the arrival of a deer. The members of the band pour onstage happily to greet the hunters and to admire the splendid deer they have bagged. As the orchestra plays "Autumn Dance," * the people dance in a circle. Finally Robin appears and rings a bell to call for attention.

ROBIN

We are going to have a feast! I'm off to fetch my lady back, and we're going to have a feast, and everyone's invited, and you're invited, and you're invited, and Hob is invited, and Little John, and Friar Tuck, and everybody is invited. I want . . .

TUCK

And me, too?

ROBIN

And you, too, Friar Tuck. Much, I want you to get me the most beautiful bunch of wild blossoms your eyes can bear.

*Music on page 197.

TUCK

And some rabbits for the stew.

ROBIN

And some rabbits for the stew.

LITTLE JOHN

Much, you can catch the rabbits, and I'll pick the flowers. (*Much rides on John's shoulders; they exit.*)

TUCK

(*calling after them*) And I'll pray for you both!

SCARLET

(*shouting angrily from offstage*) That's a lie! You know it's a lie!

ROBIN

(*as the offstage commotion fades*) Well, the sun's in the sky, the trees are in the wood, God's in his heaven, and Scarlet's in his cups, as usual. (*laughter*) I'm off now, and when I come back, I expect you to be ready with the feast, because Marion will be with me. Mix some water with Scarlet's wine, will you, Bob?

BOB

Oh, sure I will, Robin, a little water. (*Scarlet shouts again offstage and throws something. Robin sits down beside Tuck.*)

ROBIN

I can't understand it, Tuck. I can't understand Scarlet. He's a wonderful fellow, you know. (*pause*) Where IS Marion, Tuck?

TUCK

Don't worry. She's in the forest, she's on her way. (*Robin stands up and prepares to leave. He picks up a sword and a shield as Much runs in.*)

MUCH

Robin! Robin, there's a man in Richard's Meadow, Little John said the birds told him. (*He runs to tell everyone else.*) There's a man in Richard's Meadow, the birds told Little John.

ALAN-A-DALE

I'll go, Robin.

ROBIN

No. No, I'll go.

MUCH

I'll go with you, Robin.

ROBIN

No, you won't. You stay here and help with the feast. (*Robin exits; everyone shouts farewell.*)

TUCK

(*joining several men who are talking together*) She's on her way. We'll have an elegant old time of it. Like the old days. Speeches, and tricks, and a song . . . (*Scarlet enters as Tuck speaks.*)

SCARLET

(*speaking menacingly*) What did you say?

TUCK

I said, a song.

SCARLET

Don't ever say "like the old days." Do you know why you must never say "like the old days"? Because there never were any old days, Father.

TUCK

Oh, I don't know. I seem to remember a time when my mother talked quite a bit about the old days. Elegant old times they were, when . . .

SCARLET

It's a lie. It's a lie that people make up, and use, and throw it around, and do you know what they call it?

TUCK

Yes, my mother's father — that would be my grandfather — I remember that he spoke of the old days all the time, all the time.

SCARLET

(*laughing despairingly*) They call it hope! Listen to him! His grandfather! It's always too long ago to be remembered, or else it's tomorrow. (*fiercely*) It's never now. (*laughing*) Hope! (*The lights fade on him.*)

Scene vi   A Strange Duel

The metallic sound of clashing swords is heard. The lights come up on Robin and a young man dueling. The young man is hooded. Throughout the fight Robin speaks between blows.

ROBIN

Can you sing, too? Just tell me your name, boy, and what you're doing here. I don't want to hurt you. (*He speaks in time with the strokes of his sword.*) Silly sally, dilly dally, saucy soupy fig! Know that one? This is nonsense. Autumn's getting on to winter, and I don't have time to waste. I'm looking for my lady. Lovely lady with long green hair to wrap you up in when there's a chill. I shall become angry in a moment. Or two. (*He beats the young man down with blows in time with his words.*) A singer, a sailor, a joker, a jailor, danced themselves a jig! (*Robin knocks the young man's sword away. The young man is on the ground.*) Know that one?

YOUNG MAN

(*laughing*) A butcher, a baker, a Nottingham faker, cooked themselves a pig!

ROBIN

Marion! (*The strange dueler is Marion. Laughing, she pulls off her hood, and her long brown hair falls about her shoulders. Robin lifts her up and they kiss. The lights fade and quickly come up again. Robin and Marion are kissing, but now Marion is dressed in a lovely gown. Sounds of feasting and voices crying "Marion!" are heard in the distance as the lights fade again.*)

Scene vii   Marion's Feast and
the Coming of Winter

A burst of laughter and the music "Autumn Dance"* are heard. The lights come up on the entire band, assembled for the feast. There is a festive air with banners, great kegs of ale, and people filling their mugs. Robin is seated at the center of the table, facing the audience. Marion sits between Robin and Little John. A bower of blossoms encircles Robin and Marion. Other members of the band, in various postures, are seated around the table. Someone is slipping scraps of food to a dog. Hob and Ellis are wrestling on the ground. Part of a peacock's tail is visible at the periphery of the light. Steam rises from the platters of venison and fowl sitting on the table; the carcasses have much bone showing. The meal is nearly over, but people are still nibbling at drumsticks and cakes. Over the sound of laughter and music a distant bell tolls. At the moment the lights come up, Peterkin is standing on the table with three apples in his hands. Then he begins to juggle the apples, walking up and down the table with care, in and out among the place settings. He is dressed in motley and wears a bag at his side, heavy with tricks. Finally he holds out the rim of the bag. One apple in the air falls into the bag, followed by the second apple, but the third apple has magically disappeared. Now he holds in his hand a golden pear. Applause. He bows, gives the pear to Marion, and bows again for applause. He bows once more, but this time there is scant applause; he crawls off the table and begins to talk to the dog. Hob overcomes Ellis in their wrestling match. The men cheer and shout. Little John calls everyone to attention by ringing the bell. He stands and clears his throat.

*Music on page 197.

LITTLE JOHN

>(*shyly*) Now that Lady Marion is come home again, I think we should have a song. (*All cry out in agreement with this suggestion.*) The song of the seasons! (*The members of the band all sing "The Golden Pear"* * *while Marion stands at her place and beams.*)

ALL

>*Through green and gold and green again,*
>*The dawn and the midday, the nightfall and dream,*
>*Through summer and autumn, through winter and spring,*
>*We keep the wood and we seek our own king.*

MARION

>(*after a pause*) My dears, I . . . thank you. (*There is gentle laughter as she sits down. Tuck stands up and calls for attention.*)

TUCK

>Tush, now! Hush up! Everyone. (*rapping his mug on the table*) Everyone! It's time for the speeches! (*Ad-libs from the band overlap: "Speeches!" "Who's first?" "Is there any goose left down there?" "Quiet, it's time for the speeches." "Where's my mug?" "Here's a place for you, George, by me." "Shush." Gradually the band becomes quiet, except for some shifting of bodies and coughing. Silence.*)

HOB

>Well, who's it going to be? (*silence*)

ELLEN-A-DALE

>I think the lady of honor should speak first. (*Voices rise in agreement.*)

TUCK

>(*standing up quickly*) Yes. But first, I just want to say that . . . it's been so lovely, and the goose was so good, that . . . God must love you all. (*Applause. Tuck is encouraged to continue.*) I remember my mother talking about times like these; elegant times and . . . fat geese. My mother's father — that would be my grandfather . . . (*All laugh and shout him down,*

*Music on page 195.

crying for him to stop talking.) Thank you. Marion? (*Tuck coughs and sits down. Marion rises.*)

MARION

(*laughing*) Yes, I know, Tuck. And isn't it just right? And the geese were fat tonight. Just look at me. I'm getting big as a tree . . . (*laughter, shouts of disagreement*) Well, no matter. You love me, fat or thin. You know, I wasn't gone long, but now it's as if I never left at all. Oh, yes, I had a lovely visit with my father. He's lonely now, and sometimes I think he wishes he were an outlaw, so he could come live with us. But no matter. What I wanted to say was that everything is just as it was, and it always is, you know, in the forest. Your faces, and . . . oh, Robin, I can't speak. You say something. (*She sits down amid applause and cheers.*)

LITTLE JOHN

(*standing up, awkwardly thrusting Robin back into his seat*) Begging your pardon, Robin. I just want to say that . . . (*in a rush*) Marion and Ellen-a-Dale are lovely ladies. Thank you. (*The band applauds as Little John sits down in confusion and overturns a mug of ale on the table. During the ensuing flurry to wipe it up, Little John spills another mug. Laughter. Robin stands up.*)

ROBIN

A drink to you all! (*They all join in the toast.*) While me lady was gone, I had to pass the time somehow (*laughter*), so I made an arrow. (*Robin picks up an arrow and looks at it as he speaks.*) This arrow. I used the best greenwood I could find. It's the finest arrow I ever made. Believe me? Good. Well, I just knew there was someone I should give it to, and now I know who. Tonight, just before supper, I was out back in the clearing, near the old oak. Well, Much and I . . . (*People turn to Much with "oohs" and smiles. Much slides down in his seat, embarrassed.*) Much and I were practicing with the bow, and ladies and gentlemen, Much the Miller's son pulled his string all the way back to his cheek. Yes, he did! (*applause, laughter*) Even stuck his thumb in his ear to prove it! Much, this arrow is yours now.

MUCH

(*standing up to accept his arrow*) Thank you, Robin. (*Amid applause Much bows and sits down.*)

ROBIN

I don't have anything much to say. You know, it seems like time runs differently here in the wood. The green is gone, and the gold is dying. Runs faster than the brook where Little John sat me down. We'll be in winter soon. Already I hear the peacocks crying. Well, no matter. I love you all. And that's why we sit down together, isn't it, to eat and drink and talk together. For this is love's feast, and we are all of us part of love's family. (*Robin sits down. The band is quiet. The distant bell tolls again.*)

SCARLET

(*appearing from behind a tree*) Robin! Robin, may I say something?

ROBIN

Of course, Will. Always. (*The sound of crickets is heard.*)

SCARLET

Now. I mean that now I know who you are. All of you. You're so lovely. I wish I could join you. In your games, Bob. In your speeches, Tuck. But, you see, now I understand who you are. I made it up, don't you see, all of it, and now, I can't live with you. And you're so lovely, that's the shame of it. So green and so . . . good. All I wanted was a bit of green. And there you were. I remember it now. But it's like a war. No. No, it's not. It's like one man, alone, outside his own castle. And he can't get in. He hears shouts and songs . . . (*He breaks off.*) George, there, he painted that picture on the wall of St. Peter in the East. The beautiful garden in the snow. Didn't you, George? But you couldn't get in it, could you? You could never walk in those snows . . . and now, I hear the shouts and the songs, and I can't get in. To my own castle. And I've got to stop them, I can't bear it, and I'm sorry, but I can't live with it, and I've got to stop it . . . (*He breaks off and rushes out. The lights shift and darken. The people at the table slowly disappear, calling Scarlet's name; their voices blend with the moan of the rising wind. Robin is left alone at the banquet table. Only his voice can be heard in the shifting darkness, faint amid the blasts of wind.)*

ROBIN

Scarlet! Scarlet? Gone. The peacocks are crying. Forgive him. Winter. He wanted us, and there we were. He's a good man, but it's hard for him. Where is the King? By the Blessed Virgin and the Holy Child, where is the King? The peacocks are crying with the voices of men. Forgive him. Winter.

Scene viii   The Betrayal in the Snows

The violence of the storm increases and the dark woods fill with snow. The Sheriff and his men, clad in black, crouch around a fire that flickers in the high wind. Low moans are heard over the music for "The Sheriff's Song." The drunken Scarlet comes lurching through the forest. He carries a jug. A dog howls somewhere.*

SCARLET

Scarlet! Scar-let! *(more softly)* Scarlet? Where are you? *(shouting)* Where are you? Where's your dog? Wolf! I hear you. Where's your master? Scarlet! *(He lurches into the Sheriff's encampment and falls.)* Scarlet, where the hell are you?

SHERIFF

(from the shadows) Over here.

SCARLET

(startled) What?

*Music on page 195.

SHERIFF

Over here.

SCARLET

No, no! No, no! I'm Scarlet! My name is Scarlet! Who are you?

SHERIFF

(*laughing*) Come over here.

SCARLET

My name is Scarlet and my only problem is . . . I forget . . . I
forget what it is. (*spotting one of the women of the Sheriff's camp*)
What? What's that? Is that a little . . . wench? A
little . . . wench in a rug? A cold and snowy little . . . wench?
Come dance with me! (*Scarlet tries to make the woman dance with
him. A man pushes him away. The Sheriff emerges from the
shadows as Scarlet falls to the ground.*)

SHERIFF

I'm the Sheriff, Scarlet. I'm looking for Robin of Hood. Do you
know him?

SCARLET

(*laughing*) No. No, I don't know him. But I know where he is.
And I think he might be a little lonely right now. Maybe you
should visit him sometime. Maybe you should just take your
friends and go and visit him sometime. You know, it's real cold in
the woods. You know how cold it gets in the woods? (*shouting*) It
gets real cold in the woods! I'm not staying. Oh, no. Not me. Not
again. I can't do it! I can't bear it and I'm sorry, but I can't do it!

SHERIFF

Of course you can't. That's all right. You just show us where
Robin Hood lives, and we'll visit him.

SCARLET

It's all right, isn't it? I mean, it's so cold out here. You see, we
were boys together. But they won't let me in, and I can't do it any
more. I'll show you. I'll show you now. I'm so cold, though. It's
so cold out here. (*He staggers out, leading the Sheriff and his
followers through the night.*)

Scene ix   Attack

A dog barks sharply in the darkness. The members of the band, dressed in furs, are huddled in a circle around a bonfire. Hob is heard, from offstage, calling for Scarlet. Robin, Marion, and Much are at the center. They turn to face the audience, listening for the dog.

ROBIN

That sounded like Scarlet's dog. Wolf! Scarlet! I miss your ugly face, Will, around the fire.

MUCH

Robin, where is he? Why doesn't Scarlet come back?

ROBIN

I don't know, Much. Maybe he was cold. Maybe he didn't want to spend another winter in the wood. I think maybe he just got too cold. (*Several women of the band move slowly around the circle, ladling out mugs of something hot. Gradually the members of the band — first one, then twos and threes — begin to hum and to sway. Other voices join, and finally Robin starts to sing. As they sing, they rise and dance slowly around the fire.*)

ALL

All blossoms of the heath and glen
Which fill ripe summer's store
Lie fading now within the grasp
Of winter's icy shore.

All gone, now, all faded,
They rest in ice and snow.
The lady who cares for them
Will bring them life I know.

All furry beasts and finny fish
Which danced in summer's rites
Lie sleeping now in the embrace
Of winter's crystal nights.

All weary, all sleeping,
They breathe within the earth.
The lady who loves them all
Will give them springtime's birth.

HOB

(*offstage, breaking into the singing*) Robin! Robin, run! We're surrounded! (*From out of the trees evil-looking men rush into the encampment. Shouts, cries, and blows are heard. Because of the dimness of the stage and the flickering firelight, the audience cannot see clearly what is happening. A shaft of light catches Robin wielding a sword, and another reveals Marion hurrying with Much into the darkness. Finally there is silence. In the dim light several of Robin's men are seen bound to trees. The Sheriff stands in a pool of light, triumphant.*)

Scene x   Sacrifice

The bonfire flares upstage. It crackles, and its light makes the shadows of the trees move. Marion and Much are heard singing "Horses Are Running" * *somewhere in the darkness.*

MARION and MUCH
      Horses are running,

*Music on page 196.

Sleep my little baby.
Fishes are laughing
When the twilight falls.

Where is the child?
Where's the little baby?
Lying asleep,
In his own cradle.

SHERIFF

Cut it! Come out of there. Come out of there now. (*Silence. Pause. Then Much emerges, crying, followed by Marion. Another pause and then an ancient man — Robin disguised in a hooded cloak — totters out, leaning on a stick. Marion sits down at the center with Much at her knees. The old man stands behind them.*) Where's Robin Hood, old man? (*pause*) Old man, where is Robin Hood?

OLD MAN

Go away from here. Leave us . . . in peace.

SHERIFF

(*laughing*) Tell us where he is, old man. Tell us quick! (*He approaches the old man and reaches over to draw back his hood. Marion struggles with the Sheriff. Suddenly a figure dressed in green appears before the fire.*)

MAN IN GREEN

Stop! Here I am! Robin of Hood. Take me if you can. I've found my castle; these are my snows; and I cannot be touched. I am Robin the Young, Robin the Old, and I await my King! (*The man in green draws an arrow from his quiver. Robin, disguised as the old man, reaches for the Sheriff, who shakes him off and rushes to the man in green with his dagger drawn. After a brief struggle the Sheriff stabs the man in green. The man in green staggers toward Robin. He falls and dies at Robin's feet. Robin holds him and pulls back the hood; it is his old friend, Will Scarlet.*)

SHERIFF

(*indicating the men tied to trees*) Cut them loose. (*He points to the dead man.*) Pick him up. (*The Sheriff's men pick Scarlet up and carry him off. The Sheriff follows them.*)

Epilogue

ROBIN

The leaves were green, and we waited for the King. Now the leaves have fallen, and the King doesn't come back. The forest is black, and the King doesn't return. The fire was lit for the coming of the King. The fire is falling, the embers are falling . . . He was my friend. Scarlet, Scarlet. He was my friend. (*Robin draws off his hood. He is weeping. Marion goes to him, and they sit together. Much stays by the fire.*)

MARION

Do you remember when we were courting, Robin? When I still lived with my father in Malaset Castle? Before you were outlawed, before any of it? I would sit, alone in my room, and I would wait for your visits. Just waiting for you was part of it all. Knowing you would come, and afraid you wouldn't. It seems a long time ago, now. But then we came to live in the wood. And, you know, it was just the same. I would wait for the changing of the seasons, the weathers, watching for you all the while, summer and winter. I was still waiting. And now, I'm waiting again. I feel a child, Robin. We're both waiting. Come spring, I'm bearing you a child.

ROBIN

(*dully*) What? (*realizing what she has said*) A child? A baby? (*Marion laughs.*) A baby . . .

MUCH

The fire's gone down.

ROBIN

> (*amazed*) A baby! (*Robin and Marion hold each other. Much stands above them, looking down into the fire. He speaks to Bob.*)

MUCH

> I always used to watch the fire when it was going down. Of course, that was when I was little, back home. I'd lie down on the straw in front of the hearth, because that's where it was the warmest. It got so cold, sometimes, so cold, there was ice on the windows, and if my father said anything, his breath would just hang there, in the air. Outside, in the stable, steam would come off the horses, like smoke. So I'd just go inside, in front of the fire, and I'd make shapes and lands and people dancing out of the coals when they glowed. They would walk or run or just stand still, and they would say anything I wanted them to. But they never stayed. I wanted them to stay and keep on dancing. But they wouldn't. They wouldn't stay very long. They fell. When the fire died, they all fell down. (*Slowly, from the shadows, the members of the band appear, dancing slowly in the snow. They dance with upturned palms in a circle around the fire. Robin, Marion, and Much join them. They sing "The Golden Pear"* * on "la." The circle grows tighter and tighter until they are all embracing. Their laughter builds to a crescendo that ends in the thunder of drums.*)

*Music on page 195.

Robin Hood: A Story of the Forest. "Just tell me your name, boy, and what you're doing here. I don't want to hurt you." (Photograph by Bruce Goldstein.)

Robin Hood: A Story of the Forest. Robin's band dances to celebrate a successful hunt. (Photograph by Bruce Goldstein.)

Robin Hood: A Story of the Forest. A volley of arrows flew
into the clearing. (Photograph by Bruce Goldstein.)

The Golden Pear

The Sheriff's Song

Horses Are Running

Autumn Dance

Sleeping Beauty

Adapted by Richard Shaw

QUEEN
Though the winter winds may blow,
On our garden full of snow,
We will keep you from all harm
With the morning glory charm;
In a garden full of snow,
Deep down, warm flowers grow.

This adaptation of *Sleeping Beauty* was first produced by the Children's Theatre Company of the Minneapolis Society of Fine Arts in November 1971. The script was edited by Linda Walsh Jenkins with the assistance of Carol K. Metz.

Cast of Characters

Grandfather	First Good Spirit
Ben	Second Good Spirit
Susan	Third Good Spirit
Beauty	Court ladies
Prince	Geishas
Ogress	Prop men
Queen	Priest
King	Boatman

NOTE: *Sleeping Beauty* can be performed by a cast of about twenty actors (minimum) if multiple roles are assigned (for example, the court ladies might double as geishas and two prop men might play the priest and the boatman).

Sequence of Scenes

Notes on the Play

Sleeping Beauty is a tale of life emerging from death, spring following winter, and dawn succeeding dark, a theme which has its earliest roots in ancient fertility myths. In this adaptation of the fairy tale by Jakob and Wilhelm Grimm the imagery of flowers and a garden where seeds patiently wait through the winter snows conveys the underlying theme.

Grandfather, an old sea captain, narrates the story of Sleeping Beauty while the action within the story takes place in stylized Kabuki sequences. As Grandfather tells the story to Ben and Susan, the children step into some of the Kabuki scenes. The blight on life in Beauty's kingdom is personified by a terrible Ogress (played by a male actor), who becomes a giant spider that tangles the kingdom in a web of sleep. As the Prince approaches the land where Beauty lives, the Ogress challenges him with numerous trials, all of which he overcomes. When the story is over, Beauty emerges into the framing reality of the play as the children's grandmother.

The dominant Kabuki style of the play is integrated into a framework of Western elements, including the proscenium stage itself. The pagoda-roofed proscenium is flanked by two "teahouses" which are really English pavilions decorated in Japanese style. A third teahouse at upstage center is constructed and decorated in a more traditional Japanese style than the proscenium teahouses. The door of the third teahouse slides open to allow entrances and exits, and the side panels can be drawn back to reveal a painted landscape drop. The scenery is decorated with Kabuki designs and motifs from Japanese art. Various drops and curtains form the basis for major changes of scene; the prop men (who are actors in the "story") handle other scene changes. The narrative structure is Western: Grandfather, who sleeps in a very English chair by a Christmas tree, tells the story to his very English grandchildren. The audience is always aware that the Oriental scenes are the product of Western imaginations. The actors in the "story" wear Kabuki costumes, makeup, and wigs, except for the Prince, who is dressed as an English seaman. The musical score reproduces the sounds and percussive effects of Oriental music in Western instrumentation.

Prologue "Grandfather, tell us a story!"

The opening scene is a Victorian parlor at Christmas. Grandfather is asleep in his chair. Carolers singing "God Rest Ye Merry, Gentlemen" pass behind the window scrim of a painted drop. The children tiptoe in to see Grandfather.

BEN

Grandfather is asleep. He is sleeping again.

SUSAN

He's always sleeping, and on Christmas, too.

BEN

Should we wake him? (*Grandfather peeps at them, then continues to pretend being asleep.*) He'll tell us another story.

SUSAN

He looks so happy sleeping. But let's wake him anyway. (*The children tiptoe over to Grandfather, who surprises them.*)

GRANDFATHER

A Merry Chrysanthemum to ye all! (*The children are amused.*)

SUSAN

Oh, Grandfather! You were awake all the time.

GRANDFATHER

Children, there ARE tales of lands I could tell ye . . . (*The children join in saying the names of the lands in stories they have often heard.*) Singapore, Rangipur, Canton, Ceylon, Haiphong, Hong Kong . . .

205

BEN

(*with an American accent*) India!

SUSAN

(*disapprovingly and with an exaggerated British accent*) Indjhaah!

GRANDFATHER

Oh, not at all, not at all. In a land, long ago and far away, where the sun is said to rise . . . long ago and far away, even farther, even long, long ago and very, very far away . . . in a land where even the stones make songs . . . (*Susan and Ben react affectionately but negatively to the prospect of hearing another of Grandfather's tall tales.*)

BEN

Could you tell us a *true* story?

GRANDFATHER

Oh, it 'tis, it 'tis!

BEN

Tell us a true story, please!

GRANDFATHER

Well, Ben, as the great Admiral Nelson, the greatest of the great admirals, Lord Horatio Nelson, said to his English seamen . . . "England expects every man to do his duty." I will, I will tell you a *true* story.

SUSAN

Tell us how you met Grandmama! (*She pronounces the name "GrandmaMA."*)

GRANDFATHER

Ooooh, Susan. Well now, long ago and far away, where the sun is said to rise, in a land where even the stones make songs .'. .

SUSAN and BEN

Tell us how you met Grandmama!

GRANDFATHER

Well now, that's a love story, and as ye know, like all love stories, it is a bit fancy, a bit fancy, like last summer's butterfly . . . That's a tale about a flower, a flower that met me one fine day on me travels, in the auld days, in the service of our grand old Queen

Victoria . . . A very long time ago — I would say a hundred
years . . .

SUSAN and BEN

Oh no, no!

GRANDFATHER

Almost a hundred years? (*The children are silent.*) At least a
hundred years ago . . . (*The Kabuki action starts. Prop men remove the Victorian set. Grandfather and the children walk downstage and to the right of the proscenium.*) In the land of the
Chrysanthemum, where the sun is said to rise . . .

SUSAN

Oh no!

BEN

Grandpa, a *true* story!

GRANDFATHER

I will, I will. Well, you know the people here, right on this very
street, our very own street, and even in this very house: the people
here are very like the people in my true story. After all, ye know
that the sun never sets on Victoria's lands, and the people out
there, in the land where the sun rises, are just like the people here.
They had a Queen, and a King, also. But in that land the people
were a little sad, a wee bit.

SUSAN

Why?

GRANDFATHER

Because the King was rather sad.

BEN

Why was the King sad?

GRANDFATHER

Because the Queen was very sad.

BEN

Why was the Queen sad? (*Grandfather pauses, trying to decide on
the best way to develop his story.*)

SUSAN

(*helping him on with the story*) Because she had no child.

Scene i   The Magic Frog

The Queen and the court ladies enter during the following speeches and mime the action as Grandfather tells the story. The Queen performs a mime dance about a falling leaf and sadness.

GRANDFATHER

You're right, you are absolutely right . . . (*He and the children leave the stage; the remainder of their lines are spoken over an offstage microphone.*) One day, because the Queen was sad, she was working at her needlepoint, like our own fine Queen Victoria, and because the Queen was at her needlepoint, all the ladies in the land were at their needlepoint as well . . . Well, one day in the royal garden, the Queen heard a voice that might have been the voice of a prince, but it wasn't. She looked all about and saw no one. She heard the voice again, and it was a small voice. She looked and saw no one at all. She called to the ladies of the court and asked if they had heard anything and they all said, "No." And then again she heard the voice, it was a small croaky voice. She looked down and saw a frog seated upon a floating lily pad. (*A prop man draws a large frog across the stage by means of a string and places the frog in front of the Queen.*) And the Queen called all the ladies of the court and hinted, slyly, they leave so she could be alone with the frog. (*The court ladies leave.*)

BEN

Oh, Grandpa, please! Meeting Grandmother?

SUSAN

(*prompting Grandfather*) "And then I met your Grandmother, in the auld days, on me travels . . . ."

GRANDFATHER

Now, I told you, this is a love story, and that every love story is a bit of fancy . . . This tall, most handsome frog spoke honestly, truly . . . (*The Queen mimes as Grandfather provides the voice of the frog.*)

FROG

(*speaking in rhyme*)
Good morning, Your Majesty!
Wishes, wishes for a small fee!
(*The Queen nods.*)
You say you want a child?
Boy or girl, wild or mild?
(*The Queen nods enthusiastically.*)
I grant it now for *free*!
Good morning, Your Majesty!
(*A prop man takes the frog offstage. The Queen shrugs incredulously, then faints; the ladies rush in to help her. All bow to the audience and exit. Blackout.*)

Scene ii   Awaiting the Birth

GRANDFATHER

To speak the truth, I have been told,
Is to be, truthfully, a Prince. Behold —
All that has happened as that true frog foretold:

The King waited and watched and watched and waited.
The King walked and worried and worried and walked.
(*The King paces in front of the upstage teahouse. Two prop men*

*wander through, and he questions them about the impending birth.
All of this takes place in mime. Others in the court pass through,
hoping for news. The King rushes from side to side in distraction.
Finally, one of the ladies appears in the doorway of the house. All
onstage look at her expectantly, and she announces the birth by
cradling her arms. The excitement is high as the people rush to
obey the King's orders.*)

KING

Stout Soldiers, Brave Cooks: Stand to!
Mounted Messengers, Ferry Boatmen, Common Gossips:
Announce, "Beauty is born to our land!"
Actors and Artists, Gardeners and Florists:
Let a hundred flowers bloom, let a hundred blooms attend,
And all, all for Beauty!
Spinners and Weavers, Designers and Tailors,
Jewelers, Embroiderers, and you Silkworms,
Sirs*: Get busy!
Fan Makers, all Fan Makers:
Start on a fan fit for Beauty!
You have sixteen years, don't rush; do it right the first time!

Celebration, Celebration,
All Good Powers, come!
The Wise and the Foolish, Farmers, Shopkeepers,
Lords, Ladies, Samurai, Rebels, Pirates, Bandits —
Everyone, Everyone is welcome!

Celebration, Ce-le-bra-tion,
And Princes, Princes, lots of Princes,
You come too!

(*A prop man brings the King a fan to use after this long and tiring
speech. There is no blackout or other transition into the next
scene.*)

*Long ago silkworms were so important in Japan that they were addressed reverently.

Scene iii   The Christening: Blessings and an Evil Spell

Susan and Ben enter from the house, bow to the King, and participate in the action of the following speech. Kabuki actors mime the scene as Grandfather describes it over an offstage microphone.

GRANDFATHER

All across the land the happy people gathered to celebrate the birth of a lovely girl, a girl named Beauty. At the royal palace there were many, many celebrations. They planted a tree, a tree to grow with Beauty: the cherry tree, a small and formal tree. A gift, itself. In that land, one day in the spring, all the cherry trees bloom and all the people are happy, because . . . they are all a wee bit sad. Cherry blossoms are beautiful, delicate and brief. It is the cherry blossoms that make all the stones look up, rejoice, and then they sing. Many, many celebrations. And there was one most special ceremony. It was like a christening, like a christening here at home, when you were named then, Ben and Susan. It was like a christening. All the good powers of the land came; they came to give Beauty all good wishes, to give good wishes in their jeweled words, good wishes, like dew drops glistening on the morning grass. (*The court ladies bring the infant to center stage in a rose-petal cradle. All the members of the court gather in eager anticipation as two spirits with gossamer wings come to give blessings to the child.*)

FIRST GOOD SPIRIT

(*singing*)

May you have the art of the flower,

> *May you have the correctness of the plum blossom*
> *And the warm strength of the chrysanthemum.*
> (*The members of the court politely applaud her wish.*)

SECOND GOOD SPIRIT

> (*singing*)
>> *May you have the art of the flower,*
>> *The delicacy of the cherry,*
>> *The sincerity of the daisy.*
> (*Again all applaud. The Ogress enters during Grandfather's speech.*)

GRANDFATHER

> Though the King had tried very hard to invite everyone, he forgot *one* invitation: A power as beautiful as the deadly nightshade, a power as lovely and vain as the widow spider, a power as dark and wicked as a deadly Ogress. (*Shocked, everyone recognizes the Ogress and recoils from her. Susan and Ben run out of the story. The Ogress begins her "blessing." The male actor portraying the Ogress uses a falsetto voice that is at first syrupy, later harsh and eerie.*)

OGRESS

> May you have the art of the flower!
> (*Everyone is much relieved, thinking at first that the Ogress will not do anything harmful; but as the blessing turns into a curse, they become increasingly alarmed and confused.*)
>> On the morning of the first killing frost,
>> May you hang broken, wilted, brown!
>> At sixteen die, like a blasted rose
>> Or a cotton blossom, on a spindle!
> (*The Ogress departs with a grand, haughty flourish. The astonished and frightened members of the court talk among themselves, frantically whispering and gesturing as they attempt to find a solution to this unexpected crisis. The rustle of their voices is barely audible as the children question Grandfather.*)

BEN

> (*frightened*) What happened?

SUSAN

It was a curse!

BEN

What?

SUSAN

Will Beauty die, Grandfather, is it true that Beauty will die?

GRANDFATHER

No. There was, there, one more Good Spirit, but . . . she was . . . (*feeling his way through the story*) asleep in the corner . . . and that Good Spirit . . . asleep in the corner . . . had not yet given her wish. Now this beautiful and good, if a wee bit drowsy, Good Spirit did what she could. If that nightshade, that spider, that Ogress, had had her way, at sixteen Beauty would prick her finger on a spindle and she should, at once, die of that.

BEN and SUSAN

Oh no!

GRANDFATHER

But the sleepy spirit so arranged that from the loss of one drop of blood Beauty could not die, but only sleep, a long sleep, and a sound sleep, of one hundred years, until a prince would come. (*As he speaks, the third spirit rises from her place in the crowd and gently approaches the baby.*)

THIRD GOOD SPIRIT

(*singing*)

> May your sleep have the art of the morning glory;
> May it be a sound sleep, and a long sleep;
> And may you awake, dawn blossom when kissed.

(*All applaud her wish. The King thinks, scratches his head, and pulls his beard. Then he realizes the sense of the new blessing.*)

KING

Sleep for one hundred years! No! That will never do! Servants and Swordsmen, Bowmen and Huntsmen: Search out the spindles! There shall not be one spindle left in all this land! (*The court hurries away to do the King's bidding. The King and the Queen are left alone with the baby and the three ladies who hold the cradle.*)

QUEEN

> (*singing a lullaby*)
>> *Though the winter winds may blow*
>> *On our garden full of snow,*
>> *We will keep you from all harm*
>> *With the morning glory charm;*
>> *In a garden full of snow,*
>> *Deep down, warm flowers grow.*
>
> (*Blackout.*)

Scene iv   The Burning Spindles

During the blackout a drop painted to look like a blazing fire is lowered; the drop is backlighted. The members of the court stand in a semicircle downstage of the drop. They raise their arms and sway from side to side as Grandfather speaks, and their undulating hand and arm movements, silhouetted against the backlighting, suggest the flickering of flames.

GRANDFATHER

> And they gathered the spindles and the spinning wheels, and a decree went out from the King that all the spindles should be burned. And so it was; flames were seen across the land. (*Blackout.*)

Scene v   And Beauty Bloomed

Beauty enters, screened by the ladies of the court. She emerges from her entourage and performs a dance, using two large silver fans. As she dances, her fans describe symmetrical and asymmetrical patterns — swirling, curving, opening, closing; they move continuously, shining as they catch the light, always in harmony with Beauty's curving body.

GRANDFATHER
>For fifteen years the land was free of spindles, for fifteen years the land was happy, and Beauty bloomed, and bloomed, and bloomed. (*At the end of her dance Beauty bows and walks serenely to join her mother and father at the side of the stage.*)

Scene vi   The Celebration

The members of the court mime greeting one another and celebrating as Grandfather narrates.

GRANDFATHER
>And it came to pass in the sixteenth year of Beauty, the King gave a combination Celebration, Birthday, Christmas, and also Grand

Star-Viewing Party. The King often gave parties, and on that day a great star was seen in the east, and when the people saw that star, they rejoiced, with exceeding great joy.

BEN

Susan, that's the Christmas star!

SUSAN

Ssshh, Ben! That's another story!

GRANDFATHER

And the King, who was a wise King, invited all to follow that great star, invited, encouraged, ordered, whined, wheedled. He even tried poetry. "That very great star, it, too, is drunk!"

BEN

That's the Christmas . . .

SUSAN

Ssshh! That's another story! (*A silver star atop a pole is carried across the stage by one of the prop men as all the members of the court sing.*)

ALL

> *Now, when the sun is down*
> *We've the stars to watch*
> *As they turn and wheel,*
> *Until at last we're ready*
> *For dawn when blossoms wait*
> *For the stars to dwindle;*
> *Though young flowers may close*
> *On the morning glory,*
> *Yet blossoms never die.*

(*As they begin to sing the verse for the second time, the members of the court move offstage, leaving Beauty alone. The voice of the Ogress over a microphone echoes the words "wheel," "spindle," and "die." Beauty, entranced, leaves the stage in search of the voice.*)

Scene vii   The Ogress

The Ogress and the prop men step into the light and take their places.
The Ogress goes to sleep on a bench, and the prop men cower behind
and beside her. Their action does not start until Grandfather's speech is
finished.

GRANDFATHER

(*speaking over an offstage microphone*) For sixteen years, having
nothing to do but wait, the Ogress had slept badly . . . insomnia.
Now that's a bad nap. And from a bad nap, an Ogress wakes up
hungry. She'd like a live, warm, plump child to eat! (*The prop men*
force one of their number to try to wake the Ogress. He tries
several times before he is successful. Each time he sidles over to
her, taps her, then scrambles fearfully to safety near the other prop
men. Finally he awakens her.)

OGRESS

(*yawning and waking up*) Sixteen years and all bad dreams.
Dreams of princes, princesses, and True Love! (*"True Love"*
makes her choke and she coughs up a hair.) One good dream,
though . . . a dream about a fly, and I was the spider! Boys,
dress me in my disguise! (*The prop men move in a flurry to dress*
her as an old woman and to do as she wishes. They are all terrified
of her. First the wrong wig is brought, then the correct one, as the
Ogress continues to give orders.) Unbutton the dress, Cheese Lips!
Watch the nails! Watch the nails! Remove my wig! New wig!
Mirror! This is the wrong wig! Assassin! Who was that? Give me
my glasses! I want to see who that was! Glasses! Hurry! Hurry! (*A*
prop man brings her a pair of wire-rimmed glasses.) So it was

you, Squid Legs! Here, give me that! Mirror! Good! Good! Boys, how do you like it? (*They all applaud her.*) You, take that away! (*She indicates the bench; as the prop man crosses to remove it, the Ogress trips him and tries to bite him. Other prop men come to his rescue.*) I only wanted a bite of his plump leg! Boys! Boys! Let's go! (*The Ogress and the prop men exit.*)

Scene viii   Beauty Pricks Her Finger

Still entranced, Beauty enters as if drawn onstage. The Ogress enters upstage. They pause a moment in confrontation. A prop man brings a spinning wheel to the center, and the Ogress begins spinning.

BEAUTY
> (*singing*)
>> *Who are you?*
>
> (*As the Ogress sings her reply, a voice singing simultaneously with her over an offstage microphone lends an eerie, cacophonous effect.*)

OGRESS
>> *I am a kind old woman*
>> *From the far north*
>> *Of the far north wall,*
>> *Where it is always very cold.*
>>
>> *I have watched you, Beauty,*
>> *From the far west gate,*
>> *Where the sun goes down.*

Watch the wheel. It makes you warm and sleepy. Watch the

wheel. WATCH THE WHEEL! Watch . . . the . . . wheel!
(*On the last phrase Beauty reaches out and pricks her finger.
Percussion. The Ogress gleefully leaves the stage. Beauty dances
in fear, then spins madly offstage with her fans showing blood.
Prop men remove the spinning wheel and prepare the set for the
entrance of the court.*)

Scene ix   The Kingdom Sleeps

*The members of the court sing a Japanese carol to the melody of "God
Rest Ye Merry, Gentlemen."*

ALL
    (*singing*)
        All blest the cherry on the bough
        The peach, the plum, all pray:
        Remember Beauty, born and blest,
        Has bloomed this joyous day,
        And woke us all to see a flow'r
        That took our sleep away.
        Oh, blessings on Beauty, our joy.
    (*As they start the verse a second time, the action begins to slow
down. All the members of the court drowsily slump against one
another, then fall asleep. Beauty enters and tries to show her
parents the blood on her fans but realizes that they are asleep. She
falls asleep too, at upstage center, with her back to the audience.*)

GRANDFATHER
    All slept when Beauty slept: the horses in their stalls, the dogs in
the yard, the pigeons on the roof, the flies on the wall. The snails

stopped in their tracks and even the leaves did not fall. It was silent and still, as silent and still as a sleeping stone. But, the spider was weaving. The spider went on weaving, weaving at her wheel, weaving. (*The Ogress enters; overjoyed, she surveys the sleeping court.*)

OGRESS

I won. I won! *I* won! I won! I WON! Curtain! I won! (*A scrim painted with swirls of mist curtains the court, and the Ogress exits. The court is seen through the scrim; the lights on the court fade during the following speech.*)

GRANDFATHER

The flowers are all gone. This is a land of dead weeds; a land of dead weeds . . . and of spider webs. The night came, and the dawn came, and the dawn went. The winter came, and the spring came, and the spring went, and nothing in that land was fair. The cherry trees never bloomed in April. The stones slept without dreams of ever singing again in April.

BEN

Did nothing ever happen there?

GRANDFATHER

Hardly. Oh, indeed, tales were told of it, in faraway ports, as far away as Indjhaah; no one believes such tales heard in faraway ports.

SUSAN

Then those people must all sleep *forever*.

GRANDFATHER

Yes, it certainly does look that way. (*He has trapped himself in the story and is trying to think of a way out.*)

Scene x   The Prince Begins His Journey

The Prince is seen for the first time during the following speech. As Grandfather narrates from offstage, the Prince crosses in front of the gloam scrim. The lights behind the curtain are out; the audience no longer can see behind it.

GRANDFATHER

So the land slept, and slept, for at least a hundred years. UNTIL an English common seaman, a prince among English seamen, who are princes among men, he came ashore, yes, he landed in a port nearby . . .

BEN

How near?

SUSAN

Was the port asleep too?

GRANDFATHER

Hmmm. In a port nearby. He landed in a port in a nearby empire.

BEN

What kind of port?

GRANDFATHER

(*embarrassed a bit by the port activity or by his memory of it*) Well, any port . . . a port like any port . . . a sailor in every port . . . well, it was a busy port, yes, a very busy port. (*The gloam scrim opens to reveal a busy port scene through which the Prince wanders.*) And he heard such tales, such tales . . .

Of lands of golden bells and silver chimes,

Of lands where all kings spoke in rhymes.

Of latitude seven and longitude five;

Where snowflakes bloom and are alive.
Longitude twelve and latitude eight,
Where whales line up and beg for work as bait.

BEN

Grandpa!

SUSAN

Grandfather! Grandmama! (*She reminds him firmly of the story he has promised to tell them.*)

GRANDFATHER

No, no! I'll stick to God's own truth. It's how I met your grandmother, isn't it? There are such a lot of stories, such an awful lot. (*A priest enters. He and the Prince mime a conversation.*) The Prince learned, from a clergyman, from an honest priest, of the land from which all flowers fled, of the sleeping Beauty in a sleeping land, of a Beauty never kissed and waiting, waiting for a Prince from a distant land, waiting for the true kiss of an honest man. Why, he even heard that with love's first kiss, the whole land would awake, all the flowers bloom, and Beauty would arise. True Love. And the Prince said, "Veddy good!" And so the Prince set out at once, and he should have had an easy time had he known exactly where to go. "Go right at Tokyo, cross the first great water, land at the Pass of the Three Pagodas, climb the Friendly Mountain, cross the second lonely water, and land by the twisted pine; then take the straight road, The Street Without Joy, straight to the Royal Imperial Palace." (*The priest exits as the boatman appears.*) The Prince soon found a boatman to ferry him across the first great water. (*The Prince and the boatman make comic attempts to move the boat until they realize that they forgot to untie it. The boatman unties it, and they mime their exit in the boat, with the boatman rowing.*)

Scene xi   The Birds

The prop men lower wisteria blossoms from the proscenium. Several young geishas enter for a fan lesson. They make graceful choreographed patterns with their fans until the Prince enters.

GRANDFATHER

But the word had gone out, the word was carried by toads, fat toads that talked to weeds, and rank weeds that talked to spiders, and small spiders that talked to THE spider, who had once been, merely, a wicked Ogress. She spun a web of wicked plans. The first at the Pass of the Three Pagodas.

OGRESS

(her voice reverberating over an offstage microphone)

At the Pass of the Three Pagodas

My pretty little girls, my lovely geishas,

Alert! All the powers of the air, my birds,

Crow, Vulture, and Hawk,

My lovely birds, you eye pluckers,

PLUCK HIS EYES!

(The Prince enters. The geishas join their hands and move them as if they were birds' wings. Ben rushes into the story to help, giving the Prince a magic sword. As the Prince slashes at the "birds" with his sword, the geishas part their hands and let them flutter down. After all the birds have been "killed," the geishas bow and leave.)

SUSAN

How did you do that?

BEN

It was my duty.

SUSAN

So you did it.

BEN

There will be more to do.

SUSAN

I think you're right. Let's follow. (*They exit with the Prince. The wisteria blossoms are drawn up.*)

Scene xii   The Battle

The gloam scrim is drawn behind the flowers in the previous scene, and the mountain drop and the fog machine come in behind the scrim. In front of the mountain drop the prop men line up with their backs to the audience.

GRANDFATHER

Through the Pass of the Three Pagodas the Prince saw, hazy and white in the distance . . . now there's a fine sight, that mountain. Now let me tell you about that mountain. I saw it first at sunrise. That's no ordinary mountain; in that land it's more like a member of the family, always surprising you with a new view, always the same, and always changing. In that land no self-respecting artist would paint only one view of Fuji. The poets in that land call that mountain "Fuji, my friend." All of those fine people in that land say, "He who has not seen Fuji is a fool." A bit like we might say of a sailor who has not seen those white cliffs, down at Dover. "He who has not climbed Fuji . . ." (*The Prince enters with his sword in hand as the Ogress begins to cast another spell.*)

OGRESS

> (*over an offstage microphone*)
> > On the mountain, friendly Fuji-san,
> > My army drafted from the land,
> > Posts! Snow, Stone, and Steel,
> > My handsome men, you bone-breakers,
> > BREAK HIS BONES!

> (*The gloam scrim is raised, revealing the mountain and the men; the men attack the Prince with karate motions. He struggles against them as best he can. Ben and Susan rush in again to help; Ben distracts the men while Susan gives the Prince armor.*)

SUSAN

> Sir, this is the Fuji Armor of the Fog. On some days you can't see Fuji-san at all. They will not see you in the Armor of the Fog. (*The Prince puts on the armor and then shouts to the men, who cannot see him. As they turn their attention to Ben, Susan sees the danger.*) Oh Ben, Ben! (*The Prince sees the danger too and rushes in, beheading the men. Standing with their backs to the audience, the "beheaded" men perform the traditional Kabuki stage device that signifies beheading — they throw balls with red streamers into the air, and the balls tumble to the ground trailing "blood."*)

PRINCE

> For Queen and country! (*The Prince, Susan, and Ben exit. Blackout.*)

Scene xiii   The Sea Monster

The prop men enter during the blackout with two parallel painted waves. The mountain drop is pulled up to reveal a sea drop. There is a prop man at each end of the two waves. As the first wave is lowered, the one behind it is raised; together they suggest the rolling motion of waves in the sea. The Prince comes in between the waves and mimes being in a boat.

GRANDFATHER

Yes, those people say, "He who does not climb Fuji is a fool, and he who climbs Fuji twice is twice a fool." Ah well, going down a mountain is a pleasant thing, but a wee bit sad, just a wee bit. Well now, the Prince reached the second lonely water.

OGRESS

(over an offstage microphone)

At the second lonely water, near the twisted pine,
My sweet sleeper, silent, just under the surface;
Stations! Slime, Scale, Sea Snake,
My Serpent, you sinker of ships,
SINK HIM!

(A sea monster rises between the waves. The Prince and the monster fight. The Prince appears to be drowning when Susan and Ben again rush into the action. Susan addresses the audience as she appeals to British sea heroes to save the Prince.)

SUSAN

Come Nelson and Drake,
All English sea dogs,
And Grandfather too!
Drive sea monsters back

To their watery graves!

After all, Britannia rules the waves!

(The sea monster turns threateningly toward the children. The children realize that the dilemma calls for unusual action.)

BEN

Not these waves!

SUSAN

Apparently we are not in English waters! *(During the following part of Susan's plea for help, a voiceover effect is created by people offstage singing what she is saying. The Myoo she refers to are incarnations of Buddha, fierce and terrifying forms that quell men of evil nature.)*

In strange waters a stranger wish:

From the east . . . Gozanze Myoo!

From the south . . . Gundari Yasha Myoo!

From the west . . . Dai Itoku Myoo!

From the north . . . Kongo Yasha Myoo!

From the center . . . Fudo Myoo!

Bind this serpent with the sacred rope.

Change this serpent in the sacred fire.

Make him change to a swimming horse;

Be a horse the Prince can ride

On the waves, on the tide.

Be a horse that's like a fish:

It is my wish! Myoo!

(The serpent disappears beneath the waves. On the last "Myoo" the Prince emerges from the water riding a horse. He wears a costume with a horse's head in the front and a tail behind; the body fits around his waist and a long skirt falls to the ground all around. He can control the motion of the head and body.)

BEN

That's magic!

SUSAN

It was only my duty. England expects it. *(The children pat the horse and look at the Prince. As the voice of the Ogress begins to*

*intone the next threat, the horse shies and then gallops offstage
with the children following.*)

OGRESS
> (*over an offstage microphone*)
>> At The Street Without Joy,
>> On the straight road to the palace,
>> The Spider *expects!*
>> The Spider will meet you, there,
>> THERE!

BEN and SUSAN
> Wait! Wait! (*They exit.*)

Scene xiv   The Prince and the Spider

*The Ogress enters wearing a red gown; she royally commands the
center of the stage. The prop men bring in a huge golden web which
they place at upstage center as a backdrop.*

OGRESS
> Queen Weaver, King Cobweb,
> May you dream of what's polite.
> Spreading webs, spreading webs,
> On the left and on the right.
>
> (*Four pairs of prop men approach the Ogress, one pair at a time;
> each man takes the end of one of the eight lengths of red cloth tied
> around her waist and unfurls it, walking with it until it is stretched
> to its full length. Finally, a giant spider with eight long legs covers
> the entire stage and stands before the shimmering golden web.*)

Webs forever, wove about;
Spider, Spider, you're a fright,
Reaching out, reaching out,
On the left and on the right.

Webs of sleep, all about;
Spider, Spider, of the night,
Reaching out, reaching out,
On the left and on the right.

(As the Ogress is transformed into a creature preparing to fight for its life, the poetry breaks down into guttural sounds.)

Sleep forever, Beauty bright;
Spider, Spider, ah fight,
Ah uh leef, ah uh aight.

(The Prince enters but at first does not see the spider. It attacks him. A battle ensues until the Prince kills the spider. The spider withers slowly and sinks to the ground after the death-blow is struck. The prop men ceremoniously lift the spider and bear it off the stage on their shoulders.)

BEN

Is she dead? *(The Prince nods.)*

SUSAN

Is she *really* dead? *(The Prince nods again. During the next speech the prop men arrange the stage and the sleeping members of the court to look as they did when everyone fell asleep.)*

GRANDFATHER

Not really now, not really. Well, the spider was indeed dead. But how can you trust a wicked spider, especially a spider that had been merely a dotty Ogress, and a bit like the dotty Mrs. Smythe-Burns down the street. Well, the spider was indeed dead. But the Spider's Ghost . . . ah, now, that is another story. It is a bit fancy . . . but the Spider's Ghost . . . ah, yes, well and good. It is a love story, in the auld days, on me travels! It's how I met your grandmother, isn't it? There are a lot of stories, such an awful lot. Well, England expects each man to tell the truth. I will, I will.

Scene xv   The Awakening

The Prince enters as Grandfather narrates.

GRANDFATHER

Like the flowers hidden in a silent wood. Only the perfume is still lingering. Here is a brave swordsman. What a fine little lady. This one was a stout sailor. Oh, she looks like the Queen! Who ever heard of a lover sleeping? (*The Prince searches until he finds Beauty.*) Even fallen blossoms are beautiful. (*The Prince picks up Beauty's fan.*) Your fan, it must be a hundred years old. Your fan, and what good does that do? (*The Prince kisses Beauty with great melancholy. Beauty awakens, then the others awaken, and the action starts up again as if a music box had just been rewound.*)

ALL

(*singing*)

. . . *And woke us all to see a flow'r*

That took our sleep away.

Oh, blessings on Beauty our joy.

(*The Prince and Beauty promenade around the court while Grandfather narrates.*)

GRANDFATHER

And the Prince made a fine speech. He made a fine speech to the King and Queen; he made a fine speech to all the people of that land. He asked, elegantly, for the hand of Beauty, the hand of Beauty in marriage. And ye know what? They all said yes! (*The gossamer-winged spirits, who are present at the wedding, give their blessings to the Prince and Beauty.*)

FIRST GOOD SPIRIT
> (*singing*)
>> *May there be peace in the world*
>> *And tranquillity in this land;*
>> *May this land be blest with quiet,*
>> *As quiet as a garden growing.*

SECOND GOOD SPIRIT
> (*singing*)
>> *May you always hear of love,*
>> *Like gentle winds in the pines;*
>> *As a rich harvest in a rice field*
>> *May your children, grandchildren,*
>> *Always grow.*

THIRD GOOD SPIRIT
> (*singing*)
>> *May all be blest as flowers,*
>> *As radiantly warm, as comely fair;*
>> *May this last a thousand ages,*
>> *May the sun shine and never end.*

(*After the blessings and the ceremony all onstage turn toward the Prince in anticipation of a speech. He pauses a moment, then begins.*)

PRINCE
> Her Royal Highness, Victoria, Queen of England, Ireland, Scotland, and Wales, Empress of India. Our Queen Victoria . . . (*He takes out a pocket watch.*) Our Queen Victoria sends this gift to your land. This tells the time. This is the hour hand and this is the minute hand. It goes "tick, tock." (*The court applauds and murmurs "tick, tock."*)

BEAUTY
> In our land we remember as in a thousand years. How do you remember in your land? (*A prop man enters with an old-fashioned camera.*)

PRINCE
> This is how in my land we remember holidays. You must all stand

very still . . . (*The Prince arranges everyone in a pose, and they all murmur and wonder about this strange object.*) As still as if you were asleep. (*All assume a stiff Victorian pose for the photograph, and the camera flashes. Blackout.*)

Epilogue   The Prince, Beauty, and Their Grandchildren

The scene is in Victorian England again. Grandfather, Ben, and Susan enter the parlor.

SUSAN

What happened to the Princess then?

GRANDFATHER

Well, ye know, flowers bloom and grow older. That may be the art of the flower, arranging and changing. Flowers may be a wee bit like a temple bell, the sound of it ringing fades to an echo; but the bell, Beauty, she goes on and on. And a temple bell, it gets better and better. (*Beauty appears and changes into Grandmother. The prop men dress her in a shawl, mobcap, and glasses. They hand her a tea service.*)

BEN

Oh, Grandmother, we just heard about a brave Prince!

GRANDMOTHER

Well now, ye know your grandfather wanders a bit.

GRANDFATHER

Now, now! It's a long tale I've been tellin' and a long time sittin', won't you please, my dear? Won't you please?

GRANDMOTHER

Don't mind if I do.

SUSAN

And Grandmama, we heard about a Princess! A beautiful sleeping Princess!

GRANDMOTHER

Now, he does get a bit fancy, doesn't he?

GRANDFATHER

Now, now, Mother. It's a true tale I've told. You know that, don't you?

GRANDMOTHER

Well . . . *(The tone of her voice suggests that she means both yes and no.)* Forever! *(They all toast on the word "forever." The scene fades as carolers in the background sing "God Rest Ye Merry, Gentlemen.")*

OFFSTAGE VOICE

Merry Christmas, luv! *(The proscenium curtains close.)*

Sleeping Beauty. The Prince and the samurai battle on Mount Fuji.
(Photograph by Richard Paulaha.)

Sleeping Beauty. "This is how in my land we remember the holidays."
(Photograph by Richard Paulaha.)

Sleeping Beauty. In the choreography for the birthday celebration Beauty
calms two hostile samurai. (Photograph by Richard Paulaha.)

Biographical Notes

Biographical Notes

JOHN CLARK DONAHUE is artistic director of the Children's Theatre Company of the Minneapolis Society of Fine Arts. He is also an associate director of the Minneapolis Institute of Arts and serves as the Region V Governor of the Children's Theatre Association.

Donahue has written and directed the following plays. for the Children's Theatre Company: *Good Morning, Mister Tillie; Hang On to Your Head; Variations on a Similar Theme — An Homage to René Magritte; Old Kieg of Malfi; How Could You Tell?; A Wall; The Cookie Jar; The Sitwells at Sea* (in collaboration with Gar Hildenbrand); and *The Netting of the Troupial*. In addition, Donahue wrote the libretto for Dominick Argento's opera *A Postcard from Morocco* and directed the Minnesota Opera Company's production of the opera in 1971. He also wrote and directed *A Suitcase*, a play that was filmed in color by the Children's Theatre Company in 1974.

Donahue received the 1973 Arts Council Award for his outstanding contribution to the arts in Minnesota, and in 1974 he was recognized as Arts Administrator of the Year by *Arts Management*, a trade publication addressing itself to innovative management in all the arts throughout the United States.

LINDA WALSH JENKINS is currently a Danforth Graduate Fellow in the theater arts doctoral program at the University of Minnesota. She was literary editor of the Children's Theatre Company when the scripts of the plays in this volume were first assembled; later she prepared the manuscripts of the plays and related materials for publication.

Jenkins's theater experience includes acting with the Rice Players (Rice University) and study at the Dallas Theater Center and the University of Minnesota. She taught acting at the University of Minnesota and performed with the Anyplace Theater of Minneapolis before joining the Children's Theatre Company in 1969 as secretary-actress and subsequently as literary editor.

FREDERICK GAINES, who was a resident playwright at the Children's Theatre Company for two years, commutes to the Twin Cities and elsewhere from his farm home in Wisconsin to oversee or to direct productions of his plays.

Gaines has written several plays for the Children's Theatre Company: *A Christmas Carol, The Legend of Sleepy Hollow, Alice in Wonderland, Rip Van Winkle, Jerusalem,* and *Huck Finn.* He is also the author of many other plays including *The Sideshow, A Time for Heroes, The Ghost Dancer, The Stars and Stripes Forever, Wilde, Dracula, The House of Leather, Pornographic Sampler, King Solomon Is Dead, The New Chautauqua, Bull Moose,* and an adaptation of Ben Jonson's *The Alchemist.*

Gaines has received special recognition in the form of a Rockefeller Award in Playwriting and appointments as Fulbright Fellow in Theatre, McKnight Fellow in the Humanities, National Endowment for the Arts Fellow, Eugene O'Neill Fellow in Playwriting, and John Simon Guggenheim Fellow in the Arts.

TIMOTHY PETER MASON has worked with the Children's Theatre Company as an actor, a guest playwright, and a resident playwright. He also served as dean of the Theatre School for one year.

Mason has written several plays for the Children's Theatre Company: *Kidnapped in London, Robin Hood: A Story of the Forest, Musical Chairs,* and *Pinocchio.* In 1972 he received the National Society of Arts and Letters Award in the field of dramatic literature for children for *Kidnapped in London.* In 1973 he performed in Robert Wilson's New

York production of *The Life and Times of Joseph Stalin*. In addition to his activities as a playwright and an actor, Mason writes poetry, short stories, and essays.

RICHARD SHAW is chairperson of the division of liberal arts at the Minneapolis College of Art and Design. He is also a lecturer in poetry composition at the University of Minnesota.

Shaw has written two plays, *Sleeping Beauty* and *The Steadfast Tin Soldier*, for the Children's Theatre Company. He is the author of a volume of poems, *Without a Clever Title*, and he has published poetry, articles, and reviews of poetry in numerous anthologies and magazines.

ROBERTA CARLSON is a professional composer, arranger, and jazz pianist. She has composed scores for the Children's Theatre Company since 1965; she joined the staff as music director in 1969.

Carlson's compositions for the Children's Theatre Company include scores for *Old Kieg of Malfi*, *How Could You Tell?*, *The Legend of Sleepy Hollow*, *Kidnapped in London*, *Jerusalem*, *Sleeping Beauty*, and *The Cookie Jar*. She also composed scores for *Fables Here and Then*, *An Italian Straw Hat*, *The Miracle Man*, and *Bull Moose*.

SCOTT CROSBIE is a composer and a professional musician and also teaches music.

Crosbie wrote the score for the Children's Theatre Company's production of *A Christmas Carol* while he was a junior in high school. He later returned to the company to compose the music for *Johnny Appleseed*. At this time he also organized a concert band under the auspices of the Minneapolis Institute of Arts, and he wrote music for the band and its small ensemble groups.

HIRAM TITUS is a composer and a concert pianist. He first joined the Children's Theatre Company as a harpsichordist for *Le Bourgeois Gentilhomme*. Later he began composing for the company, and he also served as associate music director.

Titus wrote scores for the company's productions of *A Wall*, *Robin*

Hood: A Story of the Forest, *Spoon River Anthology*, *The School for Scandal*, *Madeline and the Gypsies*, *Hang On to Your Head*, and *Pinocchio*. He also arranged, adapted, and directed Le Petit Théâtre's production of *An Evening of Leonard Cohen*.

As a concert pianist, Titus received the New York Philharmonic Finalist Award for a young artist. In addition, he has earned awards from the National Music Teachers Association (musicianship) and from the Interlachen Press (composition).